Making Friends with the Saints

By
Therese Boucher

Pauline

BOOKS & MEDIA

Boston

Library of Congress Cataloging-in-Publication Data

Boucher, Therese.

  Making friends with the saints / by Therese Boucher.

    p. cm.

Includes bibliographical references.

  ISBN 0-8198-4826-3 (pbk.)

  1. Christian saints. I. Title.

  BX4655.3 B68 2003

  235'.2—dc21

                                    2003004750

Printed and published in the U.S.A. by Pauline Books & Media, 50 Saint Pauls Avenue, Boston, MA 02130-3491.

www.pauline.org

Pauline Books & Media is the publishing house of the Daughters of St. Paul, an international congregation of women religious serving the Church with the communications media.

1 2 3 4 5 6 7 8 9   11 10 09 08 07 06 05 04 03

To John
my companion
on the road to heaven

Contents

Introduction vii

PART ONE: Making Friends

Chapter One
　　Meeting the Saints 3

Chapter Two
　　Building Vital Friendships 21

Chapter Three
　　The Love of Every Saint's Life 39

Chapter Four
　　Spiritual Mentors in Faith 55

Chapter Five
　　Saints Come in Bunches:
　　　　The Communion of Saints 73

Chapter Six
　　What Difference Does a Holy Friend
　　　　Make? 89

Conclusion 105

PART TWO: Saintly Resources

Saints and Blesseds in Our Own Backyard .. 109

Making a Pilgrimage 115

Helping Kids Make Friends with
    the Saints 121

Websites for Saintly Friends 127

Recommended Reading 129

List of Saints Mentioned 136

Notes 141

Introduction

> The saints have no need of honor from us....
> Clearly, if we venerate their memory, it serves
> us not them. But I tell you, when I think of
> them, I feel myself enflamed by tremendous
> yearning.[1]
>
> *St. Bernard of Clairvaux (1090–1153)*

On a parish bulletin board one day in 1999, I was startled to see an announcement that St. Thérèse of Lisieux was coming to the United States and Canada. "Wait—she died decades ago!" I thought. So I searched the Internet for more information. On a web page for the National Shrine of the Little Flower in Chicago, I found this headline:

"October 5, 1999. Arrival at JFK Airport from Buenos Aires, Argentina."

Bold red letters below this proclaimed: "St. Thérèse, welcome to the USA!"[2] Even though I knew this announcement concerned her relics (sacred remains), something about the message intrigued me. The greeting seemed to suggest that somehow Thérèse was both here and in heaven. Taking this announcement literally brought all kinds of images to mind: Would there be a welcoming committee at the airport, a children's choir, a few devoted people kneeling on the tarmac? Would I want to drive the forty-two miles to JFK so I could greet her too?

I share these musings because they raise questions about the mystery we face when we take a good look at the saints. How do they relate to us on earth? Why would we want to develop a relationship with a saint? Perhaps it is because saints can guide us in our desire to know God. They are inspiring "God-lovers" who struggled with all sorts of passions. They are spiritual heroes because they went beyond failure and trusted in God's love. They are spiritual ancestors and fascinating signs of contradiction to the world around us. Most of all, our interest in them is grounded in the truth that the saints want to be our friends. But how can we meet them? And how do we befriend them?

When my father left home as a young soldier during World War II, he and my mother made a pact to pray to St. Thérèse every day, asking God, through her intercession, that he would return home safely. If he did, they promised to name their first daughter Thérèse. My father did return unscathed, and here I am as evidence of a humble saint's ability to call upon the power of God, who must have altered the flight of many bullets. I can share this book with you now because St. Thérèse befriended a newly married couple many years ago, and because of my own encounters with her and several other saints, which began when I read St. Thérèse's inspiring autobiography, *The Story of a Soul.*

Scripture refers to the saints as a great "cloud of witnesses" (Heb 12:1), a huge number of believers in the Body of Christ who have gone before us, but who continue to watch over us. The saints are spiritual sisters and brothers who have a deep affection for each of us as we struggle along life's highways. As good friends, they choose to abide with us and offer their ongoing support. The dictionary definition of "abide" gives us clues to the character of a saintly friendship: "to wait for, to accept, to endure with, to trust, and to remain stable." Friendship with a saint has a spiritual dimension that gives us new hope. As we develop friendships with particular saints, they can help us find new meaning in our day-to-day lives. Good relationships with the saints can open our hearts to more of God's love.

Let's begin the adventure of meeting the saints with a "glimpse" of heaven. Imagine standing by the water on a beach, watching clouds float across the sky, shining in the sun. As the clouds roll toward you and swell in size, you see, weaving in and out of them, figures that sparkle. A few radiant faces of particular saints dancing among the clouds catch your attention. "Since we are surrounded by so great a cloud of witnesses, let us also lay aside every weight and the sin that clings so closely, and let us run with perseverance the race that is set before us" (Heb 12:1). Let's draw closer to these fascinating and inspiring people.

> God of our ancestors who set their hearts on you.... We are surrounded by these witnesses as by clouds of fragrant incense...keep us always in their good and blessed company. In their midst we make every prayer through Christ our Lord for ever and ever. Amen.
>
> *Litany of the Saints*[3]

PART ONE

Making Friends

Chapter One

Meeting the Saints

I love New York City. For me, it is a place of spiritual pilgrimage where I encounter several of my saintly friends, especially St. Frances Cabrini, St. Elizabeth Seton, and Venerable Pierre Toussaint. After the destruction of the Twin Towers, I needed to reconnect with these saints, to understand what had ruptured the soul of our country. I decided to visit St. Peter's Church on Barclay Street, just one block from the World Trade Center. St. Peter's is the oldest Catholic Parish in New York State. It is also the church where St. Elizabeth Seton became a Catholic, and where Pierre Toussaint attended daily Mass for sixty-six years. But where were these saints on September 11? Where was God on that day? I found part of my answer in an article of a diocesan newspaper.

On September 11, a local priest, knowing that St. Peter's was closed, ran several blocks to the church and stood on the steep marble steps. He offered general absolution to firefighters as they gathered at the staging area in front of the church. Just a short time later, several firefighters laid the body of their chaplain, Father Mychal Judge, on the altar of St. Peter's church. The mercy of God was there on that day through the ministry of these two priests, in the firefighters, in workers who cared for one another, and in an invisible cloud of saints who were praying for us and who continue to do so now.

The love and protection of the saints is real if we open our eyes to their presence. A saintly friend has the capacity to be with us in good times and in bad. A saintly friend can join us in an instant and abide with us no matter what befalls us.

Discovering the presence and intervention of the saints is a bit like walking into a large room full of strangers. As you scan the sea of faces, the sight of a friend's face beckons you over. Your whole attitude toward those gathered together changes—you feel more at home and less nervous. I like to think of the Church as a room full of lively people, both visible and invisible. Each of us can be drawn into many relationships within the Church. In making saintly friends we sometimes search out a familiar face, while other times we approach someone entirely new to us and discover a wonderful, unexpected friendship. We can all become more aware of how many potential friends we have among the saints in the Church.

As a child, I was intrigued by my mother's ability to experience a spiritual intimacy with St. Thérèse, so I started to build my own relationships, through prayer, reading, and religious art, with a few saints who were "friends of the family." Later, I made a conscious effort to "make friends" with saints who faced some of the same struggles that I did. For instance, after seeing a film about St. Elizabeth Seton, who had great inner strength when she faced family illnesses and financial ruin, I could relate to her as a wife and mother. I discovered in her a new friend.

Each of us has many characteristics that may connect us to various saints. Our life unfolds in certain circumstances, such as in a small town or a large city; we may be the youngest or the oldest in our family, the only child or one of several children; we come from different nationalities and have different ancestors. Each of us has a blend of talents, shortcomings, and significant life experiences. Any of these qualities can be a good starting place in our search for saintly friends. Perhaps one of the simplest is geography.

Around the time when Pope John Paul II recommended that we learn more about saints from the Americas, our family moved from New England to the Midwest, where we lived for four years. My husband John coped with the move by building relationships in our new parish, St. Patrick's. He also delved into the parish archives and discovered Venerable Solanus Casey, OFM Cap. (1870–1957), who had been confirmed in our new parish and is a candidate for canonization. Through research at a historical library, I discovered other saints of the Americas, like St. Marguerite Bourgeoys (1620–1700), who came to the newly settled city of Montreal in 1653. She had left her home and family to become the "Mother of the Colony," educating settlers and native people alike. I also met Blessed Marie of the Incarnation (1599–1672), who was a student of St. Francis de Sales and became an Ursuline missionary in the New World. She even mastered native languages enough to write catechisms in Huron and Algonquin. Her sensitivity to children led her to provide new clothes for them and to plan celebrations with dancing, at which she played her viola.

Four years later, when we moved from the Midwest to the New York metropolitan area, where we have now lived for some time, I took the time to learn about St. Elizabeth Seton (1774–1821), a convert to Catholicism; Blessed Kateri Tekakwitha (1656–1680), a Mohawk Indian; and St. John Neumann (1811–1860), Bishop of Philadelphia. While my children learned about the social and cultural heritage of a new state, I learned about the spiritual heritage of our new home. Getting to know the saints from the New York area helped me experience an unfamiliar place as holy ground. I began to feel a new sense of belonging and appreciated the spiritual help in getting settled.

It is not a question of becoming "best" friends with dozens of saints as we move from place to place, however. Some saints you will simply nod at in passing, while you may turn to others for a long conversation from time to time, depending on what is happening in your own life. Still others can become lifelong friends. There are various kinds of relationships that you can develop according to what is best for you.

I was born around the time that St. Frances Cabrini (1850–1917) was canonized. Concern about a birth defect prompted my parents to bring me to her shrine in New York City when I was just a few months old. The prognosis was grim and included the prospect of several future surgeries on my right foot. My parents prayed to St. Frances Cabrini and promised to make an annual pilgrimage to Mother Cabrini's shrine for twenty years if my foot was healed. A few weeks after our visit to the shrine, the doctor removed the small cast I was wearing in order to prepare my foot for the first operation, and he found that it had straightened out by itself. I never needed any surgery. And St. Frances became a life-long friend of the family, whom we called upon in times of trouble, and who reaffirmed the spiritual dimension of my parents' marriage as they enjoyed what they came to call their "annual honeymoon."

It wasn't until many years later that I developed my own personal relationship with Mother Cabrini. I bought the *Travels of Mother Frances Xavier Cabrini*[1] and fell in love with her poetic way of describing the beauties of nature. She appreciated God's grandeur in the ocean, which is one of my favorite places to pray. I copied some of her most memorable comments into my spiritual journal so I could reflect and pray with them often. I also read Mother Cabrini's biography and discovered that despite her serious heart condition, she was a capable administrator, compassionate teacher, world traveler, and an untiring counselor. I felt that she understood the challenges of my job and health. When only a few people attended a class I was teaching, I remembered times when she would think of adversity as an important part of any endeavor. The fact that she lived with modern conveniences—elevators, dentures, construction companies, and even the beginnings of the Manhattan subway system— helps me feel comfortable with her and her no-nonsense kind of holiness.

> I travel, work, suffer my weak health, meet with a thousand difficulties, but all these are nothing, for this world is so small. To me, space is an imperceptible object, as I am accustomed to dwell in eternity.[2]
>
> *St. Frances Cabrini*

The Church names particular saints as patrons of occupations or areas of life. This ancient practice, which began around the fourth century, gives us models for holiness and friendship with God that are based on a saint's gifts, ministry, or interests. There is nothing like being able to talk

Nicholas, Dominic, Mary Magdalen, Ann, Joseph

about daily tasks and challenges with someone who developed similar skills. Some examples of patron saints include:

St. John of God (1495–1550), patron of nurses;

St. Anne (Mary's mother), patron of grand-mothers and homemakers;

St. Thomas More (1478–1535), patron of law-yers and court clerks;

St. Louise de Marillac (1591–1660), patron of social services;

St. Alphonsus Liguori (1696–1787), patron of people with arthritis;

St. Isidore (560–636), proposed patron of Internet users;

St. Rose of Lima (1586–1617), patron of people in desperate need;

St. Peter Claver (1580–1654), patron of Black Catholics;

Venerable Matt Talbot (1856–1925), patron of alcoholics.

St. Clare of Assisi (1193–1253) was named patron of television because she saw and heard Christmas Mass when she was seriously ill, even though she was many miles from the church. Though many saints lived in a century when current technology was not in place, the human issues they faced remain the same. You may want to choose your own patron as a spiritual friend and guardian: perhaps someone like St. Maximilian Kolbe (1894–1941) who struggled with publishing deadlines and overseeing an electrical plant, or St. John Bosco (1815–1888) who cared for homeless boys.

Your own name, a relative's name, or the patron of your parish can provide another starting place for meeting saints with whom you share a common spiritual identity. It is a centuries-old custom for Christian parents to choose baptismal names for their children that "can also express a Christian mystery or Christian virtue."[3] Parents and grandparents often feel connected to a certain saint from their culture; families have patron saints with certain qualities that loved ones want for us. Confirmation names offer another opportunity to meet the saints from your "spiritual neighborhood." God calls each of us by name, and discovering the saint behind our given name helps us discover an important part of our identity.

> Everyone's name is sacred. The name is the icon of the person.... In the kingdom, the mysterious and unique character of each person marked with God's name will shine forth in splendor. "To him who conquers...I will give a white stone, with a new name written on the stone which no one knows except him who receives it."[4]

More than once I have also been amazed by the connections we have with certain saints through the timing of important events in our lives. Our daughter Rachel, for instance, was born on the feast of St. John Vianney, and she seems to share his sensitivity to people's inner needs. My Aunt Lillie died on the feast of St. Teresa of Avila (1515–1582), an appropriate day for our family mystic who spent several hours a day in prayer.

Watching for the feast days of the saints as they come up throughout the year is a good way to get acquainted with them. You might look in the back of a Sunday missalette at the beginning of each month and choose one saint to research during the following weeks. Preparing for his or her feast day would be like asking friends about the guest of honor at a party, so that the feast day becomes a more joyous event. It is easy enough to bring a pencil and paper to church on Sunday, so you can copy the names of one or two of the saints that are celebrated that month. Then look them up in a Catholic dictionary or on a web site.

No matter which saints you decide to learn about, watch for one or two that you can feel closely connected to for whatever reason—it may not be a question of logic, geography, shared interests, or even a name; it could be a statue that catches your eye, or a book recommended by a co-worker, or a friend's enthusiastic interest. You may find that you are attracted to people who are in the news because they are at various stages in the official canonization process, like Mother Teresa of Calcutta, who has been declared "Blessed" and is awaiting the approval of a second miracle in order to be canonized. All these holy people love us, and we can grow to appreciate their love ever more. God desires to give us the support we need from brothers and sisters in Christ. St. Gregory the Great (540–604) explains the connection between believers:

> When we are linked by the power of prayer, we, as it were, hold each other's hand as we walk side by side along a slippery path; and thus by the bounteous disposition of charity, it comes about that the harder each one leans on the other, the more firmly we are riveted together in brotherly love.[5]

Though there may be many saints who attract us, God can also challenge us through saints whose actions and personalities make us uncomfortable. Saints can be paradoxes, mysteries, and signs of contradiction. One part of a saint's life may appeal to us, while another part may not. For example, St. Catherine of Siena (1347–1380) loved to cook for friends, but often fasted severely. St. Teresa of Avila, the great mystic, had visions and profound spiritual experiences, but she also wore sandals year-round and a habit of coarse serge that was occasionally plagued with lice. St. Margaret Clitherow (1556–1586) of England had a great sense of humor, but also hid priests in her home when this activity warranted a death sentence. When she was caught she took full responsibility rather than turn in neighbor and family.

The saints often become like persistent loved ones who remind us to go to the doctor or to visit a sick relative. In my own life, the words of a German mystic and writer, Blessed Henry Suso (1310–1365), have echoed in my ears as I entered a mall or a clothing store: "A detached person should always be looking to see what he can do without."[6] We all need ways to be less attached to things in order to be more attached to God. So when I am faced with an item in a store that I "can do without," I recall Blessed Henry's words and make a conscious effort to pray for the person who will buy the item instead of me.

Saints disrupt our assumptions about life— they threaten to redefine goodness and truth just by being who they are, and their actions often serve as a counterpoint to our inclinations. As we allow ourselves to draw closer to the saints we notice just how extravagant they are in their love for God. It is almost embarrassing to hear them talk about their own sinfulness and their overpowering desire to please God above all else. Don't be alarmed if you have to catch your breath sometimes! A saint's voice can echo the inner voice of God who is calling you to new levels of friendship within the Body of Christ, and ultimately with himself. You will find new strength to face those challenges if you let the saints show you what you need.

St. Luke's Gospel recounts a story about two disciples on their way to Emmaus after the crucifixion (24:13–35). They met a stranger on the road and expressed their discouragement about the death of Jesus. The stranger's conversation gradually eased their worries, until finally they realized that the stranger was Jesus. Then they exclaimed, "Were not our hearts burning within us as he spoke!" With the help of the saints, God will stir up the Holy Spirit within us and assist us in realizing his promises in ever-deepening ways. Like the disciples on the road to Emmaus, we must have the courage to let "our hearts burn within us" as we meet Jesus.

Meet a Saint

Saint Juan Diego (1500s)

Juan Diego was a native of Mexico whose indigenous name was Cuauhtlatohuac, which means, "The Eagle Who Speaks"—and he certainly speaks to us down through the ages. One winter day, during his daily fifteen-mile walk to Mass, Mary appeared to Juan as a pregnant Aztec woman surrounded by golden rays of light. She asked him to request that a church be built on that spot, so that people could experience her as their compassionate and devoted mother. Juan went to the bishop with her request. The bishop, however, needed more evidence of the truth of Juan's story.

Mary appeared a second time and told Juan to gather into his cloak (tilma) the fresh roses that were growing nearby, and to present them to the bishop. Juan did as he was asked. Once again he went to the bishop and when he allowed the miraculous, out-of-season roses to tumble to the floor, they both saw imprinted on his tilma the beautiful image of Our Lady of Guadalupe, which remains to this day. This image and Juan's experiences challenge us to set our hearts on the reality of heaven, and to be open to ongoing revelation from God.

If you have a diary or a spiritual journal, use it to get in touch with God and with a saint you would like to befriend. Introduce yourself by writing him or her a short note. Try to think of one inspiring quality about this saint and end by thanking your new friend for his or her example of faith. ∼

Choose one of the saint's quotes or Scripture passages in this book. Put the quote on a piece of paper and place it on the refrigerator or put it in a daily planner. Repeat this quote to yourself several times throughout the week. Spend some time praying about these words and how they have touched your life. ∼

Prayer Sampler

St. Francis of Assisi (1882–1226)

All praise be yours, my Lord, through all
    that you have made,
and first my lord Brother Sun,
who brings the day; the light you give to us
    through him.
How beautiful is he, how radiant in all his
    splendor!
Of you, Most High, he bears the likeness.

All praise be yours, my Lord, through Sister
    Moon and Stars;
in the heavens you have made them, bright
    and precious and fair.
All praise be yours, my Lord,
    through Brothers Wind and Air,
    and fair and stormy,
all the weather's moods, by which
    you cherish all that you have made.[7]

Litany of Saints

Venerable Solanus Casey, you greeted streams
of anxious people who came to the friary door
and offered them God's peace. Pray for me as I
wait in lines, in traffic, in restaurants and stores.
Help me to focus on God's presence and receive
God's peace. Father Solanus, pray for me. ∼

St. Rose Philippine Duchesne, you gladly surrendered a comfortable life to embrace struggling pioneers, yellow-fever patients, and the poor.
You had a lifelong desire to work among Native
Americans, but didn't get permission to start
until the age of forty-nine. Pray for me as I face
my limits. Pray for me when my dreams are too
small. ∼

St. Elizabeth Seton, you were always willing to seek more of God's love, even if it meant suffering discrimination because you were Catholic. Pray with me when I feel afraid to profess my faith and to witness to God's presence at work or in public places. ∿

I repeat your prayer:

My God and my all! Save, save, that I may return you an Eternity of gratitude and praise.[8] My refuge, let not my frail nature shrink at your command. Let me say, Lord, here am I, creature of your will, rejoicing that you will lead, thankful that you will choose for me.[9]

Chapter Two

Building Vital Friendships

> There is no harm to the saints if their faults
> are shown as well as their virtues; great harm
> is done to everyone by the hagiographers who
> slur over the faults, be it for the purpose of
> honoring the saints…or through fear of dimin-
> ishing our reverence for them.[1]
>
> *St. Francis de Sales*

In the summer of 1992, my husband and I
decided to add a short pilgrimage to our family's
vacation agenda and traveled to the Shrine of the
North American Martyrs in Auriesville, NY. Only
a few miles away was the excavated village of
Blessed Kateri Tekakwitha, "Lily of the Mohawks,"
who was born in 1656. She interested me because
of a distant ancestor named Anne Mouflet, who
married an Onondaga Indian in 1697. Both Kateri
and Anne Mouflet were part of the Iroquois na-

tion. We read Kateri's biography together in the car and attended her feast day liturgy in Auriesville. We stood next to the village stream and imagined what it was like for Kateri, as a young Indian maiden, to carry heavy pails of water back and forth, and then to come to know these waters as the fount of new life through her Baptism. Our young daughter Katie liked the fact that Kateri "babysat" and wore a blanket over her head to protect her weak eyes from the sun, and she has developed a long-term relationship with Kateri since then.

"Open wide the doors of our hearts to Christ." John Paul II extended to us this invitation in his first greeting after becoming pope. Most of us need lots of spiritual support to attempt such a project; we need someone to point out inner doors that may be unexplored or locked or rusted shut. The saints can be spiritual friends and guides who are like doorways to a new and deeper life with God. Getting to know them is a way of experiencing how any one of us—no matter our personalities or problems—can draw closer to God. In the saints, we have real brothers and sisters in Jesus Christ who struggled with building an intimate relationship with God and loving people in their daily lives. For instance, Blessed Andre Bessette (1845–1937) often found himself snap-

ping at the multitudes of visitors who sought
healing. St. Jerome (340–420) struggled with a
bad temper. And St. Jane de Chantal (1572–1641)
experienced great inner struggles during her life
of faith. In her writings she describes forty-one
years of grave uncertainties, doubts, "spiritual
nausea," depression, and qualms of conscience.
Yet each of these saints, despite their human
struggles and even failings, triumphed in coming
to know God and growing in their lives of faith.

Developing deeper relationships with the
saints means learning about their lives—their
personalities, gifts, and struggles. Each saint
stands as a unique witness, a sign of hope that
will increase as we work on building a friendship. Growth toward intimacy with a saint involves
thinking about what we have in common: life-
changing events, talents, emotional concerns. It
means facing what seems to be beyond us, such
as a saint's intimacy with God—acknowledging
that each saint's focus is on God first is integral
to this friendship. And developing an intimate
friendship means taking the time to talk to the
saints frequently, using simple conversation, lita-
nies, and prayer. Sometimes we can share a mo-

ment with a saint just by recalling something we have in common.

During my first silent retreat, I used reading and painting as ways to be with God. I brought a book about St. Thérèse that included biographical sketches, quotes by St. Thérèse, Scripture verses, and suggestions on how to pray. Each morning, I painted a landscape in response to the beauty of trees, birds, or the clear waters of a small pond. One morning, I remembered that St. Thérèse herself also enjoyed drawing and painting. I felt as if she was sitting beside me, painting a nearby rose bush, and sharing a particular tube of red paint. Thérèse's smile and her silent friendship were very affirming. St. Thérèse reminded me that God wants to be very involved in every detail of our lives—leisure, family, and personal problems. God wants to enter our lives, to sit beside us. Jesus wants to be our constant companion. The Holy Spirit is as close as a heartbeat and as constant as the act of inhaling and exhaling. Saint Thérèse had ushered me into a new and deeper joy as with her I experienced God's creative love.

Many of the saints themselves spent time studying and praying for the intercession of the saints who lived before them. St. Francis de Sales

(1567–1622) was the bishop of Geneva who led many to God through his *Introduction to the Devout Life.* He advises us: "Make friends with [the saints]. Talk with them frequently, using words of praise and tenderness."[2] St. Ignatius Loyola (1491–1556) was brought to faith by reading the lives of the saints, and St. Edith Stein (1891–1942) was converted by reading the works of St. Teresa of Avila. St. Thérèse of Lisieux contemplated ways that she could be like the martyrs. She especially admired St. Bartholomew the Apostle, St. Joan of Arc, St. Agnes, and St. Ignatius of Antioch.

St. Joan of Arc (1412–1431) was herself guided in a very concrete manner by her relationship with the earlier martyrs, St. Catherine of Alexandria and St. Margaret of Antioch. Perhaps experiences with saints can give one new ways to trust God when "uncharted" spiritual territory is explored. St. Thérèse, for example, lived during a time when many people focused on God's justice and making restitution or payment for sin, but she held onto a strong conviction about the tender mercy of God. *"How can I fear a God,"* she kept asking, *"Who is nothing but mercy and Love?"*[3]

Friendship with the saints often requires effort on our part because they lived so long ago, or because they came from cultures unfamiliar to us—and they are not physically present to us like our other friends. How many of us can relate to the legend of St. Patrick dealing with a beach full of snakes? What could we have in common with someone like St. Edith Stein, who faced death in Auschwitz? How many can identify with St. Vincent Ferrer, whose preaching was accompanied by hundreds of miracles?

Because Pope John Paul II has beatified and canonized many persons from the twentieth century, we now have many saints who are more accessible to us through photographs, printed materials, and even video footage. We don't have to delve into past centuries or wander far from home in our search. This pope has given us hundreds of new examples of holiness from every corner of the globe, which means that almost every job, every geographic place, and even modern culture can potentially be something that we share with these new spiritual friends. And sharing the particular details of daily life makes us feel more at ease with them and all that they offer us. It can also bring new levels of meaning to our experiences, which may be similar to theirs. Someone like Blessed Gianna Beretta Molla

(1922–1962), for example, faced the sobering issue of abortion both as a doctor and in her own pregnancy. She understands the many medical decisions that have moral and ethical consequences.

By looking closely at the saints' lives, we can begin to understand the contexts of their faith and appreciate their responses—and we can see that they are truly human. When we take the time to step into each saint's world, then the human issues he or she faced become clear. We can glimpse the way a particular saint surrendered to God's Spirit, even when it meant a great deal of suffering. For many, this surrender came only after a profound conversion experience. For others it meant responding to God in ways that were ahead of their time or unacceptable in their society.

St. Thomas More (1478–1535), for example, refused to take the oath required of all subjects, which declared King Henry VIII's marriage to Catherine not lawful. For this Thomas was condemned to die, but his thoughts on death were just as revolutionary as his actions. In a commentary about Jesus in the Garden of Gethsemane, he explains that it is only normal and even prudent to be afraid of death. We should not feel guilty about our fears. St. Thomas believed that

Bonaventure, Peter Claver, Andrew, Felicitas, Perpetua

Jesus had been "immeasurably more frightened" than he was at the prospect of his own execution. He realized that the challenge we face is focusing on Jesus and not letting our fears drag us into a lack of trust in God's love. Both St. Elizabeth Seton and Venerable Pierre Toussaint (1766–1853) lived in New York at a time when Catholics were openly harassed and discriminated against. For Pierre, this meant living an unassuming life of quiet philanthropy. For Elizabeth, it meant facing the threat of having her home burned and fleeing to Baltimore in order to build Catholic schools.

> [The saints] contemplate God, praise him and constantly care for those whom they have left on earth. When they entered into the joy of their Master, they were "put in charge of many things." Their intercession is their most exalted service to God's plan. We can and should ask them to intercede for us and for the whole world.[4]

When we are in trouble and searching for a way out, God can seem very far away. We need someone who can act as a bridge to God. This is when an intimate relationship with a saint can come into play. Asking a saint for help is like that first call to a nearby neighbor or friend, whose presence and support gives us the courage to face whatever challenges or difficulties confront us. In this way, saints can sustain and guide us through our troubles.

We are often tempted to replay all the details of a problem until our feelings grow larger than life as we lament the situation. It is far better, however, to turn these laments into prayer. We first have to remember that we have friends who want to help us. We are not alone. We can tell God and the saints about all the pain and emotion that we are experiencing. Sometimes we would rather run away than face our difficulties, but telling God how we feel is important. A story is told about St. Teresa of Avila, who was tossed out of a wagon when the wheel came loose. As she lay in the mud, maybe with a scowl on her face, she said, "Well God, if this is the way you treat your friends, no wonder you have so few of them." The important thing is that she thought of God right away and began to give the irritation, shock, or whatever other feelings she was experiencing to God.

God and all the saints are more than willing to listen to our troubles. They are always bending down to help us when we fall. The saints stay with us throughout our whole lives, beginning with the celebration of the sacrament of Baptism, which includes a litany to the saints. When we pray this litany, it is as if the saints are gathered around the baptismal font like proud relatives. Even when we die, our funerals will end with the prayer, "Saints of God, come to [our] aid! Come to meet [us], angels of the Lord! Receive [our] souls and present [us] to God the Most High...."[5]

Once I had a very painful case of hives that lasted several days. I was sore and exhausted from lack of sleep. One night I prayed to several saints at once and imagined them standing around my bed, pouring jars of lotion on my skin. As I prayed, I became aware of God's presence, too, and the word "strawberries" came to mind. It was a silly thought because I am allergic to strawberries and know I shouldn't eat them. But the thought persisted, so I reviewed everything I had eaten that day. I thought of a new vitamin supplement I had been taking, so I got up and inspected the label, which indicated that the first ingredient was manufactured from strawberries. I am not quite sure how, but I believe that these saintly friends were instruments of God's healing and wisdom. Their love brought me a peace of mind that allowed me to see the situation in a new light.

To this day, I keep a collection of saints' cards on my nightstand and glance through them when I am having trouble. Sometimes it is easier for me to think in pictures than in words, so just looking at their familiar faces helps me know that their love is enduring. Of course, some of my favorite saints have a way of migrating to the top of the pile and staying there for a while!

An important part of turning to the saints for help is appreciating the attention we have received from them, even before any help is evident. We can expect the saints to continue praying for us even after we have finished describing our situation. We can also expect God to hear them. We might end our prayer of petition with an "Our Father" or a few lines from a psalm as a way of turning our thankful attention directly toward God. Thanking God immediately does not mean that we stop struggling with our feelings or cease desiring the intercession of the saints. It means that we recognize the source of a saint's ability to help us. A saint's love is a sign of God's love, the same God who is always beckoning us to become aware of new thresholds of God's ever abiding presence. St. Thérèse of Lisieux describes the movement of our hearts and minds when we pray.

Prayer means the launching out of the heart toward God. It means lifting up one's eyes, quite simply, to heaven, in a cry of grateful love, from the crest of joy or the trough of despair. It is a vast supernatural force, which opens out my heart and binds me close to Jesus.[6]

We can only begin to imagine the things that will happen when we are willing to gather ourselves into God's presence, when we join his holy saints and angels in the great adventure that we call prayer. St. Catherine of Genoa (1447–1510) had a vision of enormous warehouses in heaven. When she asked God what they were for, he told her that they were filled with all the gifts and blessings he wanted to give his children. But no one had ever come to claim them. God listens. God is waiting. The more often we draw near to God, the greater will be our transformation. Let us join the saints and angels in praising God despite our troubles. There are no "reserved" seats in the presence of God. Praying *to* the saints means praying *with* the saints. It means being surrounded by our friends and feasting our eyes on God together.

Sing to the Lord, all the world!
Worship the Lord with joy;
come before him with happy songs!
Acknowledge that the Lord is God.

He made us and we belong to him;
we are his people, we are his flock....
Give thanks and praise to him.

(Ps 100:1–3a, 4)

Meet a Saint

Venerable Pierre Toussaint (1766–1853)

Born into slavery on a plantation in Haiti, Pierre is the first black person from the United States to be formally recognized as "Venerable" by the Church. He is also the only layman interred in the crypt below the altar in St. Patrick's Cathedral in New York City, where Archbishops and Cardinals are laid to rest.

Toussaint, a slave of the Berard family, was more fortunate than other slaves, since he knew how to read and write. After learning the art of hairstyling, he became well-known for his fine skill, and wealthy New Yorkers frequently sought him out. Pierre used the money he earned to free other slaves, rather than buying his own freedom. After his master's death, he discreetly supported the Berard family with his earnings. His master's widow finally granted Pierre his freedom on her deathbed. By then, Pierre was a well-to-do professional, and he married Juliette Noel. He walked to daily Mass at St. Peter's Church in Manhattan for sixty years and offered financial aid, shelter, and encouragement to orphans, poor refugees, priests, plague-stricken people, and weary travelers. Besides providing ongoing funding for the Prince Street Orphanage established by St. Elizabeth Seton's sisters, Pierre also helped raise money for the construction of St. Patrick's Cathedral in Manhattan. Instead of retiring from his lucrative coiffure business, he kept working well into his eighties because, he said, "Otherwise, I would not have enough for others." The priest who delivered his eulogy said, "There are few left among the clergy superior to him in zeal and devotion to the Church [and] among laymen, not one."[7] And isn't that who we are too, lay men and women, not canonized saints, just people who try to love and serve from one day to the next?

Saints are examples of "heroic virtue" lived out in a particular time and place. Their inner lives are marked by ongoing conversion. They let God shape and reshape their thoughts, emotions, and actions. Think about struggles that have taken "heroic" effort to deal with in your life. Write a letter to God or to one of the saints about one of your struggles. End your note by asking for a saint's help. Then write a litany of "thank-you" prayers for specific things that have gone well in your life. ∼

The psalms include many laments about all kinds of trouble. Look at Psalm 42, 63, or 22, which Jesus prayed on the cross. Write a lament of your own by rewriting one of these psalms around a particular situation you face today. Tell your favorite saint about your difficulty, and then end by reading a thanksgiving psalm like 8, 100, or 145:1–9. ∼

Prayer Sampler

St. Ignatius of Loyola (1491–1556)

Lord, I freely yield all my liberty to you.
Take my memory, my intellect, and my entire will.
You have given me anything I am or have;
I give it all back to you to stand under your will alone.
Your love and your grace are enough for me;
I shall ask for nothing more.[8]

Litany to the Saints

St. Thomas More, you served God as a law-yer, but took the time to build a good life for your family. You educated your daughters, led family prayer, and even enjoyed playing with a pet mon-key. But when it came time to choose between God and king, you risked all of this. Help me sort out what is really important at work and at home. Help me give everything and everyone to God. St. Thomas, pray for me. ∼

Blessed Kateri Tekakwitha, you took Jesus as your one love and enjoyed nothing more than talking with him in the forest. Poor eyesight and family opposition did not keep you from pursu-ing a life of prayer, penance, and service. At your death you whispered, "Jesus, I love you." In death, the joy and beauty on your face inspired hun-dreds of people who came to your funeral. Help me fall in love with Jesus too. Blessed Kateri, pray for me. ∼

Venerable Pierre Toussaint, you refused to gossip about others or to diminish the dignity of either the rich or the poor. Help me see each person in my life through the eyes of our merciful savior, Jesus Christ. Pray with me, Pierre, as I examine my own attitude toward those whom God puts in my path each day. ⌒

Chapter Three

The Love of
Every Saint's Life

My friend Mike has decorated his office with some impressive pieces of artwork, but in the midst of all this art is a small bulletin board with an old, tattered prayer card of St. Frances Cabrini. When I asked him about the picture, he told me about his first teaching job at a Cabrini high school. Mike wasn't a Catholic, but as he studied Mother Cabrini's life with his students, he began to develop a friendship with St. Frances. That year brought a deep conversion of life and a hunger to participate in Sunday liturgies. Mike eventually became a Catholic due to his friendship with Mother Cabrini.

Like each of us, saints inhabited an everyday world that perhaps included various places and relationships: home, work, family, church. An appreciation for their daily life can only enhance our friendship with the saints, as well as give us a guide for understanding our own worlds. When we compare our world with theirs, it helps us examine what is at the center of our lives. Each of us must ask, "What is at the heart of my world? How does the heart of my world differ from that of a saint's world?" I remember the time my young daughter fell against the corner of a rocking chair and needed stitches in her forehead. As I stood beside her while the surgeon worked, Katie kept her eyes glued on my face. I was her hope, her lifeline, just like the psalmist looked to God: "To you I lift up my eyes…. As the eyes of servants look to the hand of their master, as the eyes of a maid to the hand of her mistress, so our eyes look to the LORD our God" (Ps 123:1–2). What is our focus in life? What has evolved into a lifeline for us? Is it a spouse, a relative, a career goal, or words of wisdom from a friend?

Reading any saint's biography, one soon discovers that the most important person in every saint's life is Jesus of Nazareth. Saints are "God-lovers" who give us the best possible view of their Beloved and wish to share that view with us—we just have to look closely. What the saints behold in Jesus is like a treasure at the core of our spiritual heritage, and can be our greatest source of inspiration. By knowing Jesus in a particular, but universal way they have added to the human family's intimacy with Father, Son, and Holy Spirit.

For instance, the saints have given flesh to various names and titles of Jesus. Jesus has been their Shepherd, their Brother, their Redeemer. St. Catherine of Siena (1347–1380) experienced Jesus both as "Beauty Supreme" and as the "Loving Madman" who risked both the Incarnation and the cross in order to save us. St. Bernard of Clairvaux (1090–1153) knew him as "honey in the mouth, music to the ear, a shout of gladness in the heart."[1] St. Ambrose (340–397) saw all goodness as contained in Jesus:

> When we speak about wisdom, we are speaking of Christ. When we speak about virtue, we are speaking about Christ. When we speak about justice, we are speaking of Christ. When we speak about peace, we are speaking of Christ. When we speak about truth and life and redemption, we are speaking of Christ.[2]

This desire to experience Jesus and to seek his presence is often evident in the way the saints prayed, and their insatiable hunger for God drove them to their knees. In God's presence some of the saints experienced contemplation, visions, and prophetic messages that give us glimpses of

Jesus, and they shared these revelations with the world. St. John Vianney (1786–1859) once described this all-consuming desire for an intimate relationship with Jesus.

> My Jesus…all the world cannot satisfy the immortal soul. It would be like trying to satisfy a starving person with a grain of corn. It is good when we set our hearts, our imperfect hearts, on loving you, my God. We were made for [love].[3]

A saint's capacity for knowing Jesus in prayer is evidence of an absorbing love affair with God that weathers periods of dryness in prayer and a lack of consolation, as well. The saints did not always have easy or rewarding experiences, and not all of them experienced "revelations." But they persisted in seeking God's presence. St. Monica (332–387) alternated between faith and worry during the thirty years that she prayed for her son, Augustine, before she finally saw the fruits of her persistence in his conversion. St. Rose Philippine Duchesne (1769–1852) spent several decades praying and asking to be a missionary. She was seventy-one before she finally realized her dream of ministry among Native Americans. Though she was unable to teach, she felt great joy in praying to Jesus for the Potawatomi people. She prayed so often that they called her the

"Woman Who Prays Always." The saints remind
us that God will give us whatever gifts we need
to experience an ongoing, prayerful relationship
with Jesus.

Of course, the saints are involved in much
more than gazing at Jesus. They also move from
prayer to action, imitating the love and service of
others that Jesus practiced. St. Paul reminds us
that all Christians are called to imitate Jesus and
to pattern our lives on his. Jesus often went by
himself to a lonely place in order to pray, but
then he returned with a plan of action. We too
can draw strength from the Father, the Son, and
the Holy Spirit and then take it into the world
through our words and actions every day.

Scripture is an important place where we can
grow in an understanding of God's point of view
and learn to put it in action. Blessed Pope John
XXIII (1881–1963) reminds us, "Let us meditate
on the Gospels. Amidst the confusion of so many
human words, the Gospel is the only voice that
enlightens and attracts, that consoles and quench-
es thirst."[4]

Some saints found themselves radically
changing their lives because of the words of Scrip-

ture. In his autobiography St. Augustine (354 – 430) describes an experience he had while torn between his desire for God and his struggle with sin. Feeling great anguish, he was sitting under a tree when he heard a voice saying, "Take and read!" Augustine opened the nearest book at hand, the Bible, and found a passage in Romans that said, "Let us live honorably as in the day, not in reveling and drunkenness…. Instead, put on the Lord Jesus Christ, and make no provision for the flesh" (Rom 13:13, 14). Those words burned into his soul, and moved by a profound grace, he experienced a deep peace and a lasting conversion. Even though his struggles continued, he persisted in reading the Scriptures. He once said: "Learn to fix the eye of faith on the divine word of the Holy Scripture as on a light shining in a dark place until the day dawns and the daystar arises in our hearts."[5]

Many of the saints found that the Scriptures not only guided them, but also described their journey of faith. One aspect of Scripture could become like a "theme song," a way to live out their own love for Jesus. Saints often felt attracted to a particular part of Scripture or to an aspect of the life of Jesus. Some desired to imitate Jesus in his preaching, such as St. Dominic (1170–1221), St. Francis Xavier (1506–1552), St. Isaac Jogues

(1607–1646), and St. Francis de Sales. St. Isaac
Jogues was so convinced of the scriptural call to
bring God to the whole earth that, though he left
Canada after being tortured and maimed, he decided to return to Quebec to continue serving
there. Francis de Sales gave spiritual direction to
lay people and encouraged a love for Jesus in the
Eucharist when the practice of staying away from
Sunday liturgies was widespread. "Whoever turns
to [the Eucharist] frequently and devoutly so ef-
fectively builds up his soul's health that it is almost impossible for him to be poisoned by evil
affection of any kind."[6] Many saints, such as the
Apostle Paul or St. Edith Stein (1891–1942), chose
the suffering and the cross of Jesus as their focus—his passion gave meaning to their lives. St.
Bernadette Soubirous (1844–1879) once said, "O
Jesus! Jesus! No longer do I feel my cross, when
now I think of yours!"[7] She reminds us that we
have a companion in the midst of our difficulties
and a Savior no matter how overwhelming our
situations may be.

The suffering of the saints is often empha-
sized by the nature of the canonization process,
since one of the criteria for canonization is "heroic" virtue, and virtue seems most heroic in the
light of suffering. Virtue and holiness may re-
quire something like the proverbial furnace in

which to be refined and purified. And it is common for saints to view their sufferings as opportunities to draw near to God, because they have a deep appreciation for the whole Paschal Mystery. St. Faustina Kowalska (1905–1938) offered her sufferings for the conversion of those trapped in sin and prayed: "I will lock myself up in the most merciful heart of Jesus. I will bear my own sufferings in silence."[8]

Others sought out the suffering people around them and embraced the cross of Christ by embracing others. St. Elizabeth of Hungary (1207–1231) once put a desperately sick leper in her own bed. When her irate husband pulled back the covers he saw the crucified Jesus. How easy it is for us to be so self-absorbed that we don't even give a second glance to a person in need. Perhaps we are often like Elizabeth's husband, who needed to be challenged to see beyond the surface and love the unlovable. Suffering is not the final reality, but it can help us to appreciate God's love and communicate that love to others.

The choices that the saints have made challenge us to make choices, not only to love Jesus, but also to love *as* Jesus loved. St. Edith Stein reminds us that it is very important to "learn to live at God's hands" and to bring God's love to those around us.[9] The lives of the saints illustrate this process of reaching out in love. They responded to every imaginable form of human suffering, drawing from the vast storehouse of God's unbounded love for us. The saints have loved God's people in ways that reflect God's mercy. Like Jesus, they acted out a compassion that flowed from and was energized by prayer. Blessed Pauline of Mallinckrodt, Germany (1817–1881), expressed this strength when she prayed, "Lord, help me be a soul of prayer; help me that all my works swim in prayer."[10]

Saints are compassionate examples of the corporal works of mercy: they fed the hungry and gave drink to the thirsty; they clothed the naked and sheltered the homeless; they visited the imprisoned and the sick; they buried the dead. They made God's love visible, often spending themselves in a lifelong call to ministry.

St. Martin de Porres (1579–1639) is an example of self-giving, prayer-filled compassion and love. One of the first saints to be canonized from the Americas (Peru), he was the son of a Spanish nobleman and a black native who became a third order Dominican. He did the most humble jobs in the monastery, but was best known for his service to the sick and the poor. St. Martin collected monetary donations each week to provide food, clothing, medicine, and shelter for the poor. The monastery in Lima became a soup kitchen, clinic, and homeless shelter. He sought out those in need throughout the city of Lima and beyond, often carrying food and clothes to destitute soldiers in a seaport five miles away.

We also have the example of St. Margaret of Scotland (1046–1093), who used her position as a queen to feed, clothe, and shelter hundreds of people. During Lent and Advent she and her husband daily served food to 300 people in the royal hall. Blessed Damien de Veuster (1840–1889) responded to all the human needs of the lepers he served on Molokai. Even though he struggled with his revulsion at the smell of rotting flesh, he dressed wounds, built houses and orphanages, made coffins, and raised money for the needy.

Saints also have eyes to see deeply into the human soul and a capacity to respond to the spiritual needs of God's people. Because they have a heightened spiritual consciousness, they can address the most profound needs of the human spirit. They follow Jesus in his ministry to the human heart and mind. Their lives are filled with spiritual works of mercy that include instructing the ignorant, admonishing the sinful, counseling the doubtful, praying for others, comforting the sorrowful, and forgiving wrongs. Blessed Peter To Rot (1912–1945) persisted as a catechist in Indonesia and defended the sacrament of Matrimony even though it cost him his life. St. Katharine Drexel (1858–1955) worked to reverse the effects of racial prejudice in the United States. St. Maximilian Kolbe took a prisoner's place in the death bunkers of Auschwitz and spent his final days comforting those who would die with him. Blessed James Alberione (1884–1971) with Venerable Thecla Merlo (1894–1964), founded the Pauline family to proclaim the word of God through modern technology and communications media: radio, film, television, books, magazines, software, and Internet.

Each of these saints invites us to love our neighbor on every level. The saints have loved by ministering to others with the heart of Jesus, and in turn, they challenge us to a "saintly" and "heartfelt" response to those around us. The saints invite us to surrender to God's tremendous love and to rely on this infinite source of strength in order to transform the world. Venerable Thecla Merlo encourages us to accept this invitation, to imitate Jesus, and to serve:

> It is hard to become saints, but we don't want to give up the idea just for that. Let us work

steadily, with faith, and in the best way we know how. God sees. God is a good camera-man, and at the Judgment he will project the film. See to it that you are good stars—shining stars.[11]

Meet a Saint

St. Edith Stein (1891–1942)

Edith Stein was born on the feast of Yom Kippur, the Jewish Day of Atonement in Breslau, Germany. She rejected her family's religion as a teenager, and her university studies only seemed to confirm her atheistic convictions. She earned her doctorate in philosophy and became a prominent philosopher and author. Edith was impressed by an encounter with a Christian friend's widow who faced her loss with calmness. "It was then that I first came face to face with the cross and the divine strength which it gives those who bear it."[12] The turning point of her conversion experience came when she read the autobiography of St. Teresa of Avila. Teresa's words touched a deep chord in Edith, and she could only react by saying, "This is truth!"

Her desire to become Catholic brought her family great pain. Her mother wept bitterly when Edith told her of her decision. But St. Edith considered her conversion a return to her Jewish roots. She once said, "My return to God made me feel Jewish again." She thought of her relationship to Christ as existing "not only in a spiritual sense, but in blood terms,"[13] referring to her heritage as one of God's Chosen People. Edith spent the next twelve years translating important Catholic books, lecturing, and writing. She became a Carmelite at age forty-three and devoted the rest of her life to prayer and writing. When the Nazis gained power, and the persecution of the Jews escalated, Edith fled to a Carmelite monastery in the Netherlands, but found even that country was not safe. A few days before she was arrested, she responded to the nuns' pleas that she flee again by saying, "Why should I be spared? Is it not right that I should gain no advantage from my Baptism?"[14] She died in a gas chamber in Auschwitz on August 9, 1942.

There are many names and images used to describe Jesus that come from Scripture, including:

Emmanuel, Chosen One, Lamb of God, Prince of Peace, Son of David, Suffering Servant, Good Shepherd, King, Living Bread, Savior, Son of Mary, Christ, Healer, Messiah, Lord, Bridegroom, Just One, Word of God, Light of the World, Redeemer, Image of the Invisible God.

Choose one or two names that appeal to you and one or two that you find challenging. Think about how you might grow in faith by addressing Jesus with these names. Use one of these titles to begin a journal entry that describes Jesus. Reflect on this title and how it has shaped your relationship with Jesus. Repeat the name slowly as a prayer. ∿

Take some time to think about the life of Jesus. Imagine yourself sitting by the Sea of Galilee listening to Jesus. Describe what you can see, hear, smell, and touch. What is Jesus saying to the crowd or to you? If you were to make your way over to him, what would happen between you? What event in the life of Jesus speaks to you the most? What does it say about who Jesus is and what he is calling you to be? Describe your encounter. ∿

Prayer Sampler

St. Clare of Assisi (1193–1253)

Happy the soul to whom it is given to attain this life with Christ, to cleave with all one's heart to him:

Whose beauty all the heavenly hosts behold
    forever,
Whose love inflames our love,
Whose contemplation is our refreshment,
Whose graciousness is our delight,
Whose gentleness fills us to overflowing,
Whose remembrance gives sweet light,
Whose fragrance revives the dead,
Whose glorious vision will be the happiness
    of all the citizens of that
    heavenly Jerusalem.
For he is the brightness of eternal
    glory (Heb 1:3), the splendor of
    eternal light.[15]

Litany to the Saints

St. Katharine Drexel, you spent your inheritance establishing missions for Native Americans and African Americans. But, even more important, you gave yourself with joy to God and his people. Help me surrender myself to Jesus, so I can also say, "My dying is eternal life with Christ. To the extent which I comprehend Christ in faith, to the same extent I shall embrace him with love."[16] St. Katharine, pray for me to become a lover of Christ. ∼

St. John Eudes, you forgot yourself in order to serve the sick and the outcast members of society. You called those around you to trust in the Sacred Heart of Jesus. Help me to make your words my own, "Jesus is my All, and I desire to belong to him, wholly to him. It is the most extreme folly and delusion to look elsewhere for any true happiness."[17] St. John, help me choose Jesus. ∽

St. Thérèse of Lisieux, you knew Jesus as both Savior and beloved Spouse. Help me see the face of Jesus. Help me to fall more in love with Jesus today and each day of my life. St. Thérèse, your passionate love for God led you to declare, "You cannot be half a saint. You must be a whole saint or no saint at all."[18] I want to become a saint; help me remain faithful to Jesus. ∽

Blessed James Alberione and *Venerable Thecla Merlo,* you had a passion for using the media to proclaim the Good News of God's kingdom. Help me see the many opportunities I have to bring the Good News of Jesus to others, so that I may respond to their physical and spiritual needs. Help me spread God's love. ∽

Chapter Four

Spiritual Mentors in Faith

Certain saints have become important to me almost by accident. After driving our son Tim to college in Baltimore, my husband and I stopped at St. John Neumann's shrine in Philadelphia. After seeing the saint's personal belongings—handwriting samples, cherished books, a chalice, and even the stone doorstep where he collapsed and died—it seemed appropriate to ask St. John Neumann to help Tim, who had been born on his feast day. Over the next few months I prayed to St. John about my son's growing discontent at school, and that he might find housing near the college. Tim finally found a good apartment near the campus, and only one block from where St. John Neumann had lived in Baltimore. That's when I realized that this unassuming bishop was paying attention to me. Tim and I had a new friend.

The first thing I learned from this experience was to let go of my son, just as the Neumann family had to let go of theirs when he left for America. After all, I realized, God loves Tim more than I do. Another thing I realized was that St. John Neumann, like Tim, had experienced several dead ends in his search for the right approach to what he wanted to do, so he would understand Tim's situation. By reading St. John Neumann's biography I learned about the importance of humility and honesty in praying for family members.

The word "disciple" derives from a Greek word meaning "learner." When we build ongoing relationships with God's saints, there is always more to learn. We become students of these saints, for when we set out on the road as followers of Jesus, we need guides who know what lies ahead of us. We need saintly mentors, who become like coaches, wisdom figures, companions, and protectors who point the way to Jesus. These mentors can help us to honestly say to Jesus, "Let me be like your disciples on Mount Tabor, seeing nothing else but you, my Savior."[1]

If we read the Scriptures carefully we notice that a large group of disciples followed Jesus. Like Jesus, many of the saints also had disciples during their lives, and are willing to mentor us today as well. Some saints established religious orders and lay institutes that still offer support and guidance for people today. We are also fortunate to have many of the saints' primary documents as a source of learning and inspiration. No matter how we pursue a life of faith, an insatiable thirst for holiness, learning, and spiritual growth mark a disciple of Jesus and the saints. This thirst for greater holiness along the road of life radiates from the words of St. Frances Cabrini:

> This will be my main interest, the purpose of all my steps, my comings and goings, all my preoccupations, of all that comes my way in work; to love Jesus, to seek Jesus, to speak of Jesus, and to make Jesus known.[2]

The Church has numerous ways of learning from the many kinds of saints. Certain titles are given to different saints—such as martyr, mystic, apostle, doctor, confessor, founder. These designations are clues to what we can learn from them.

Since martyrs are saints who have given the ultimate witness by giving up their lives for God, they can teach us something about the direction our lives might be taking and about the ultimate message that each life presents to the world. Some saints became martyrs because of one dramatic event, but martyrs are saints because of the way they lived their whole lives. St. Ignatius of Antioch, St. John Perboyre, St. Margaret of Clitherow, St. Perpetua, and St. Thomas More not only died because of their faith, but they lived that faith until their deaths. Martyrs did not usually give their lives suddenly, in one moment, although it may seem that way. Their lives unfolded through a series of choices made without regard for personal security. St. John Perboyre, for example, decided to be a missionary at the age of fifteen and volunteered for ministry in China at a time of intense persecutions. Near the end of his life he endured twenty different interrogation sessions without betraying other Catholics in China. The martyrs can teach us about our choices and can reassure us as we face the many little deaths that are a part of daily life, and the compromises that are a part of the relationships that we build with others. They offer lessons that apply to the most serious situation that we will all face: death. Although we may not be called upon to die for our faith as were St. Thomas, St. Margaret of Clitherow, or St. John Perboyre, we can gain the courage to die to self by serving others and witnessing to Jesus though our actions. St. Thomas More's prayer prompts us to look at

the direction of our whole life and our ultimate
destiny.

> Give me your grace to amend my life and to
> face my own death without grudge or fear,
> for to those who die in you, good Lord, death
> is the gate to a wealthy life.[3]

Mystics are recognized for an unusual intimacy with God. These saints help us dream big
when it comes to prayer, showing us that it is
possible to fall in love with God and to experience great depths of joy and meaning in his presence. St. Bonaventure (1218–1274) advises us,
"When we pray, the voice of the heart must be
heard more than the proceedings of the mouth."[4]
St. Catherine of Siena once heard God speak about
the experience and the result of prayer:

> I can love you more than you can love your-
> self and I watch over you a thousand times
> more carefully than you can watch over your-
> self. The more trustfully you give yourself up
> to me, the more I shall be watching over you;
> you will gain a clearer knowledge of me and
> experience my love more and more joyfully.[5]

Mystics offer us the inspiration we need to
base our lives in prayer. Their prayer experiences

encourage us to open the inner doors to our hearts. Sometimes we can learn how to pray by reading their spiritual diaries and their descriptions of personal encounters with God. Many mystics, such as St. Teresa of Avila, Blessed Julian of Norwich (1342–1413), St. Paul of the Cross (1694–1775), and St. John of the Cross (1542–1591), even left us some specific guidelines and instructions about the spiritual life.

Founders and foundresses are like arrows aimed at the truth about who God is for us, offering clarity and understanding about the Gospel, the Creed, and leading a Christian life. For instance, many of us face important decisions that affect how we will live our faith and how we will embrace our vocation to serve others—like choosing a job, buying a car, joining an organization, or selecting a place to live. These undertakings can be a means for us to open our hearts to the ongoing direction of God in our daily lives and to seek God's help when obstacles arise. We can learn such trust and discipleship from St. Frances Cabrini, foundress of the Missionary Sisters of the Sacred Heart, who had a strong fear of water that stemmed from a near drowning when she was seven years old. Yet she endured twenty-three international ocean voyages. Nothing would deter her from doing what God had asked of her. Early in her ministry, Jesus had promised her, "I (will) protect and guide you with my hands from one sea to the other."[6] After that, Mother Cabrini experienced a deep, lasting peace as she traveled for the sake of her immigrants.

Doctors of the Church (such as St. Jerome, St. Augustine, and St. Thérèse of Lisieux) not only teach us profound theological doctrines, but are also like "spiritual health professionals" who show us how to live as followers of Jesus. Saints have used the image of sickness to describe our constant need to choose God and seek healing and forgiveness before we take a new direction in life. St. John Chrysostom (347–407) called sin the "ulcer of the soul." These saints are evangelists and master catechists who "doctor" us by helping to reshape our attitudes and judgments about life. They teach us to focus on God and the fulfillment of our baptismal promises—they know what it means to reject sin, to believe in God our Creator, to love Jesus our Redeemer, and to live in the Holy Spirit. These baptismal promises have impacted all the experiences and details of the saints' lives and shaped their thinking on the nature of reality.

As our world becomes more complex, it is significant that Pope John Paul II has given us St. Thérèse of Lisieux as a Doctor of the Church. Her simplicity in living out her Baptism is just what we need to counterbalance the complicated challenges of materialism, terrorism, and managing information through global computer technology. In a letter to her sister Marie, St. Thérèse wrote:

> What pleases God in my little soul is that he sees me loving my littleness and my poverty: it is the blind hope that I have in His mercy. That is my only treasure. Why can it not be yours? To love Jesus, the more one is weak… the more one is suitable for the operations of [God's] consuming and transforming love. It is confidence and nothing but confidence must lead to love.[7]

As we learn about God from the saints, we can also learn a great deal about ourselves. We can learn about the vocation God is calling us to, and discover personal weaknesses, charisms, and gifts. Just as we see and learn about elements of ourselves in a saint's life or work, we may be able to identify with a particular saint's spirituality or approach to God. Often we can discover and adopt these spiritualities. The *Catechism of the Catholic Church* expresses the importance of these spiritualities:

> In the communion of saints, many and varied *spiritualities* have been developed throughout the history of the churches. The personal charism of some witnesses to God's love for men has been handed on.... The different schools of Christian spirituality share in the living tradition of prayer and are essential guides for the faithful. In their rich diversity they are refractions of the one pure light of the Holy Spirit.[8]

Such spiritualities can give meaning and direction to our particular gifts, insights, and relationships. Within these spiritualities we can often find a place to grow and be formed. A spirituality can be as simple as a recurring "theme song" or style of prayer that shapes one's personal relationship with God. It can punctuate the events and activities of daily life, and becomes a familiar starting point for a sustained spiritual life. A spirituality can also be a whole school of spiritual thinking and guidelines for living. The following are examples of some spiritualities and the saints that espoused them:

The Little Way

As an assistant novice mistress, St. Thérèse of Lisieux was a spiritual mentor for several sisters in her convent. She encouraged poverty of spirit in her sisters, and she invites all of us to let go of self in order to please God. Thérèse once explained, "Remaining a little child before God [means]…not to become discouraged over one's faults, for children fall often, but they are too little to hurt themselves very much."[9] The spirituality of "the Little Way" focuses on spiritual childhood and gratitude for God's personal love and mercy. St. Thérèse prompts us to place everything in God's hands and to strive to grow in trust.

Compassion for the Poor

St. Elizabeth of Hungary, St. Vincent de Paul (1581–1660), St. Katharine Drexel, St. Francis of Assisi, and Blessed Mary McKillop (1842–1909) from Australia are among the many saints who expressed their "spirituality of compassion" through ministry to the poor. St. Vincent de Paul, for example, created organizations to serve the poor and orphaned in France. He formed the Sisters of Charity, an order dedicated to caring for the sick and the poor. Vincent and many others sought out the poor and embraced them in love by helping them both materially and spiritually.

"My all for Jesus"

Many spiritualities are centered on the person of Jesus and accepting a radical call to follow Jesus. For instance, St. Ignatius Loyola chose the motto, "For the greater glory of God." He once said, "Man was created to praise, do reverence to, and serve God our Lord and thereby save his soul."[10] From this focus he developed the Ignatian spirituality, one of the most prominent spiritualities centered on Christ. St. Paul of the Cross focused on the redemptive love of Jesus.

Another expression of a Jesus-centered spirituality is based on devotion to the Sacred Heart of Jesus. St. Margaret Mary Alacoque's (1647–1690) revelation of the personal love of Jesus was a major factor in spreading in the Church this insight into God's love for us. This prayer of hers helps us reflect on the promises that are a part of God's intimate and personal love:

> Hail, Heart of my Jesus: save me!
> Hail, Heart of my Creator: perfect me!
> Hail, Heart of my Savior: deliver me!…
> Hail, Heart of my Master: teach me!…
> Hail, Heart of my Pastor: guard me!
> Hail, Heart of my Brother: stay with me!
> Hail, Heart of my Incomparable Goodness:
>   have mercy on me!
> Hail, most loving Heart: inflame me. Amen.[11]

Conversion and the Kingdom

Some saints, such as St. Patrick and St. Francis de Sales, discovered a missionary vocation that sprang from a spirituality of conversion and dedication to the kingdom of God. A passion for conversion and radical obedience is evident in St. Augustine as well, for he prayed: "May I humble myself and exult you. May I think of nothing except you. May I die to myself and live in you."[12] St. Catherine of Siena is another example of someone who lived this type of spirituality. She promoted reconciliation between rulers, popes, and ordinary people. One day as she prayed for two hardened murderers being brought to their deaths, both saw visions of the Crucified Jesus and repented. These saints can help us choose God and pursue an ongoing conversion that will keep faith from becoming a lukewarm enterprise.

Marian Spirituality

For some saints, drawing ever closer to Mary was the aim of their spirituality. They teach us to rely on her as a spiritual mother who helped them to know God. Some of the saints who had a profound devotion to Mary include St. Dominic, St. Louis de Montfort (1673–1716), St. Maximilian Kolbe, St. Bernadette Soubirous (1844–1879), and St. Catherine Laboure (1806–1876). Bernadette was a poor farm girl from Lourdes who encountered the Blessed Virgin in a grotto. Mary introduced herself as the Immaculate Conception. After the apparitions ended, Bernadette devoted herself to a quiet life of prayer. St. Catherine Laboure also experienced visions of Mary, who revealed to her a vision of a small medallion, which came to be known as the Miraculous Medal. At Mary's request, St. Catherine had thousands of medals made, and the devotion quickly spread. St. Catherine told no one except her spiritual director that she was the "Sister of the apparitions" until shortly before her death. She lived a quiet life of prayer and service in a hospice as a Daughter of Charity.

We can discern our spiritual identity through study, prayer, journaling, and seeking spiritual direction. Our spirituality is not usually something that we can determine on our own. St. Teresa of Avila is a fine example of someone who was willing to often seek guidance to discern what God was doing and saying in her life. She approached her spiritual director or confessor with real detachment from her own religious experiences. As the story goes, many of her insights were messages that she heard as spoken by God, but she would present them as insignificant ideas, so that her spiritual director was free to accept or reject them.

The communion of saints spans centuries and far-off places, and in order to develop a spirituality and live a balanced Christian life that is appropriate for today, we often need guidance. Fortunately, we can turn to our Christian friends today to sort things out. Shared prayer, study, celebrating the sacraments, and participating in faith-sharing are important ways of staying connected to the Christian community as we explore the lives of Jesus and the saints. When we imitate the saints in prayer and devotion and follow their examples of service to others, we will make progress in the spiritual life and we will grow in a personal spirituality. St. Alphonsus Liguori reminds us to rely on God for the grace to persevere as we follow Jesus:

> Grant me the gift of knowledge, so that I may know the things of God and, enlightened by your holy teaching, may walk, without deviation, in the path of eternal salvation. Grant me the gift of counsel, so that I may choose what is more conducive to my spiritual advancement.... Grant me the gift of wisdom so that I may rightly direct all my actions, referring them to God as my last end.[13]

Meet a Saint

St. John Neumann (1811–1860)

John had a quiet childhood and enjoyed spending time engrossed in reading, astronomy, and botany. He had good grades in the seminary and had such a flair for languages that he could speak six fluently. (He would know twelve by the time he died). After completing his studies, he chose service in the American missions rather than a comfortable ministry in his native Czechoslovakia. He set out for America with one small trunk, a scribbled address, a dollar, his rosary, and devoted trust in "our Blessed Lady." Ordained in New York City, John cared for scattered immigrants along the East Coast. During his twenty-four years as a priest, he walked hundreds of miles and traveled by stagecoach, barge, horseback, sleigh, and wagon to reach those under his spiritual care. His passion was being among his people. In order to be well-grounded in prayer and community, he joined the Redemptorists in Pittsburgh and pronounced his religious vows "before our Blessed Lady...and the whole court of heaven."

Fr. John did not want to be a bishop, but when called to that service, he embraced the opportunity it gave him to build hundreds of grammar schools and establish Forty Hours Eucharistic devotion in the diocese of Philadelphia. A high point in his life was a trip to Rome for the definition of the dogma of the Immaculate Conception of Mary in 1854. Bishop Neumann was chosen by the pope to serve as book bearer during the ceremony. For St. John, having this honorary role was a sign of Mary's love for him. St. John Neumann died on the eve of the Epiphany while doing errands and praying the rosary.

Reflect on the saints and spiritualities presented in this chapter. Choose one that attracts you and write a letter to God about this saint and his or her spirituality. Write about your desires to follow Jesus and what you might learn from this one saint. Ask for help with the obstacles that you face in pursuing this kind of spirituality. ∽

Just as each person has unique fingerprints and a unique voice, each of us has a "theme song"—an approach to God, a unique way of relating to the One who is above all and in all. But we can also share a spirituality with other Christians and with the saints. Think of a hymn that says something important about your identity before God. Pray with this song for a few days, letting it echo in your heart and mind. ∽

Prayer Sampler

St. Richard of Chichester (1197–1253)

Thank you, Lord Jesus Christ,
for all the benefits and blessings
which you have given me.
Merciful Friend, Brother, and Redeemer,
may I know you more clearly,
love you more dearly,
and follow you more nearly, day by day.[14]

Litany to the Saints

Mother Mary, Spouse of the Holy Spirit, pray for us. ⁓

St. Ambrose, courageous and holy before God, pray for us. ⁓

St. Patrick, zealous to speak God's word to those who had not yet heard the Gospel, pray for us. ⁓

St. Francis of Assisi, lover of all creation, pray for us. ⁓

St. Francis de Sales, pastor and teacher, pray for us. ⁓

St. Bernadette Soubirous, ever humble in God's presence, pray for us. ⁓

St. John Vianney, pastor of God's family, pray for us. ⁓

St. Catherine of Siena, lover of the Church, pray for us. ⁓

St. Margaret Mary Alacoque, devoted to the Sacred Heart, pray for us. ⁓

St. Edith Stein, daughter of Abraham, pray for us. ⁓

St. Ignatius of Antioch, freely spending your life for God, pray for us. ⁓

St. Joan of Arc, courageous in following God's directions, pray for us. ⁓

St. Cyril of Jerusalem, alive with God's Spirit, pray for us. ⁓

St. Margaret Clitherow, passionate about the needs of the Church, pray for us. ⁓

St. Maximilian Kolbe, lover of Mary Immaculate, pray for us. ⁓

St. Augustine, believer in the mercy of God, pray for us. ⁓

St. Louise de Marillac, compassionate and care-filled lover of the poor, pray for us. ⁓

St. Martin de Porres, lover of the poor, pray for us. ⁓

All you holy saints and angels, pray for us. ⁓

Amen.

Chapter Five

Saints Come in Bunches: The Communion of Saints

On one recent All Hallow's Eve, when my husband and I heard a knock at the door, we were greeted not by the usual "trick or treat," but by the total silence of a black hooded figure with a long beard and a flashlight. The mysterious guest was attending our annual "All Saints" party, where everyone dresses up as favorite canonized saints. During the evening, besides lots of food and fun for everyone, each member of the group takes turns asking two "Yes or No" questions of each costumed saint, with prizes awarded for guessing a saint's identity. Our silent guest was one of the most challenging saints at that party. He turned out to be St. Sharbel Makhlouf. None of us had ever heard of him, but we learned a lot that night. Sharbel (1828–1898) was a Lebanese

Juan Diego, Martin of Tours, Teresa of Avila, Alojzije Stepinac, Patrick, Jacinta

hermit who had taken a vow of silence and devoted himself to a life of holiness and contemplation, especially before the Blessed Sacrament. After his death he became widely known for a bright light that emanated from his tomb for forty-five days, which beckoned people to prayer at the monastery. Many who came to pray at the tomb were healed; many also experienced a renewed love for God.

Every year, our All Saints party represents a microcosm of the communion of saints, stretching back through time and drawing from every continent and culture. The gathering helps those who attend gain a new appreciation of the saints and become acquainted with a few more friends in the Church. But an All Saints party cannot begin to portray all the saints we could celebrate. Multitudes of holy people march through history right into the present day. We come from a very big family with countless sisters and brothers in Jesus. The blend of human and holy that goes into imitating just a few of them on All Hallow's Eve makes me feel more at home not with just a few saints but the whole crowd.

By canonizing some of her faithful...the Church recognizes the power of the Spirit of holiness within her and sustains the hope of believers by proposing the saints to them as models and intercessors. "The saints have always been the source and origin of renewal in the most difficult moments in the Church's history." Indeed, "holiness is the hidden source and infallible measure of her apostolic activity and missionary zeal."[1]

The canonization process is founded on the idea that it is possible to love God and neighbor to a heroic degree—and we have inspiring, universal examples of how to do so. It is important to keep in mind that the Church does not "make" someone a saint through this process. The Church merely recognizes what God has done and is still doing through a particular person. The whole canonization process is meant to reaffirm God's activity in every age, place, and time:

Step one: A person's life is reviewed by the local diocese. If the findings are positive, then the person's "cause" becomes official and the Vatican declares this person to be a "Servant of God." Several people from the United States are in this category: Bishop James A. Walsh (1867–1936), Mother Henrietta Delille (1812–1862), Mother Marianne Cope (1838–1918), Mother Maria Kaupas (1880–1940), and Bishop Frederic Baraga (1797–1868).

Step two: The documentation from step one is then passed on to the Vatican and the Church's Congregation of the Causes for the Saints, which continues the investigation. Because of heroic virtue and a "reputation of sanctity that is authentic, spontaneous (without fraud), constant (from death to the present), and enduring (continues to grow),"[2] the person is declared Venerable and his or her body is located and inspected in order to verify his or her identity. Catherine McAuley (1778–1841), Cardinal Terrence J. Cooke (1921–1983), Cornelia Connelly (1809–1879), and Pierre Toussaint are examples.

Step three: The Church requires a miracle obtained through the intercession of the holy person. The miracle gives evidence that the person is in heaven and testifies to his or her holiness of life. All miraculous claims are subjected to rigorous scrutiny by medical and theological experts. In the cause of Blessed Pope John XXIII, a pediatric nurse named Sr. Caterina Capitani was near death in May 1966, after surgeons removed three-fourths of her stomach. As the sisters in her congregation prayed for the intercession of Pope John XXIII, she received a vision of the recently deceased pope and was healed. When a miracle like this is approved, the person is beatified (declared Blessed) and public worship can be offered on a feast day that is set within this person's country or region.

Step four: After an additional miracle is approved, the person is declared a saint, although occasionally the pope will waive the second miracle requirement. In Elizabeth Seton's case, for example, canonization came after only one approved miracle in which a construction worker recovered from a serious accident. After canonization, a feast in honor of the saint may be celebrated throughout the universal Church.

Two very different songs celebrate the unity between the saints in heaven and those of us on earth. One is the traditional hymn, "For all the Saints" by William Howe, which speaks about the communion and fellowship that is a part of God's plan.[3] Another is the contemporary Christian song "Circle of Friends" by Douglas Kaine and Steve Siler, which refers to all of us as one great circle of compassion. This connection is so real that "when we meet in heaven we will recognize each other."[4] Both songs hint at an even more amazing truth: the unity of the communion of saints is a reflection of the love, intimacy, and compassion that exists in the Trinity among the Father, Son, and Holy Spirit. God is the ultimate communion of persons, and all the saints, living and deceased, are drawn into the life of the Trinity. God is the source of compassion, love, and oneness. St. Paul expresses what happens to all those who surrender to the love of the Trinity:

> For this reason I bow my knees before the Father, from whom every family in heaven and on earth takes its name. I pray that, according to the riches of his glory, he may grant that you may be strengthened in your inner being with power through his Spirit, and that Christ may dwell in your hearts through faith, as you are being rooted and grounded in love. I pray that you may have the power to comprehend, with all the saints, what is the breadth and length and height and depth, and to know the love of Christ that surpasses knowledge, so that you may be filled with all the fullness of God (Eph 3:14–19).

Scripture and Tradition offer us many images for the Church community: the Body of Christ, the People of God, the Bride of Christ, the branches of a vine, the family of God, the flock. St. Ambrose called the Church the "safest harbor of salvation for all in distress."[5] During their lives on earth, many saints lived out these images of Church and faith community by seeking other holy people and building friendships, such as John Neumann and Blessed Francis Seelos (1819–1867), or St. Francis of Assisi and St. Clare. St. Augustine received direction and help from St. Ambrose. St. Katharine Drexel sought the advice of St. Frances Cabrini. St. Elizabeth Seton describes the connection between believers in this beautiful passage:

> Link by link the blessed chain: One body in Christ—he the Head, we the members. One faith—by his word and his Church. One Baptism—and participation of his sacraments. One hope—him in heaven and eternity…. He above all, through all, and in all. Oh, my soul, be fastened link by link, strong as death.[6]

For many saints, the call to live in a community of love is seen concretely in their choice of living in religious communities. Though we may not be called to this particular vocation, we can still see in their lives reflections of our own humanness, though it is lived out in a different setting. Whatever our calling in life, a commitment to our faith community is at the root of all Christian vocation—community is meant to be a crucial part of our lives as Christians. We need to work at choosing God together with other people. An active participation in our faith community is the most helpful context of a saintly life, since the community's support and even its faults often helped many saints grow in their capacity to love. We must ask ourselves how we, too, can share in the life of our faith community in one of the many ways available.

One of my favorite stories about living in community involves Blessed Kateri Tekakwitha. After several years of harsh treatment in her village because of her Christian beliefs, she fled to a community of Native American Catholics in Quebec. There she met a woman who had been her mother's friend and who had guided Kateri in her faith after her mother's death. Kateri was blessed through her friendship with a person who had been a part of her own spiritual heritage, in addition to finding herself surrounded by a new community of faith-filled people.

Like Kateri, many of us must seek out a spiritual family, whether it is a Bible study group, a gathering for family prayer, a daily liturgy community, a prayer group or rosary gathering, or a parish faith-sharing group. We need brothers and sisters, fellow pilgrims and saints, to help us stay on the road, for it can be much too difficult to follow Jesus alone. St. Teresa of Avila describes what we can do as we support one another and as we become the Body of Christ:

> Christ has no body now on earth but yours…
> yours are the eyes through which Christ's com-
> passion looks out at the world; yours are the
> feet with which he is to go about doing good,
> and yours are the hands with which he is to
> bless us now.[7]

> All the sacraments are sacred links uniting
> the faithful with one another and binding
> them to Jesus Christ, and above all Baptism,
> the gate by which we enter into the Church.
> The communion of saints must be understood
> as the communion of the sacraments.[8]

The presence of the saints is an important part
of our worship and we acknowledge the many
holy women and men who pray alongside us
whenever we gather. Statues, stained glass win-
dows, feast days, and prayers during the Eucharistic celebration remind us of their presence. The
Church's ancient practice of keeping relics of
saints, especially martyrs, can be seen as an invitation to encounter God in sacramental community, as well as in the faith community. Having
relics as well as other sacramentals reminds us
that we join the saints in praising and worship-
ping God when we celebrate the sacraments.

Our friendship with the saints can inspire us to celebrate the sacraments with greater fervor. St. John Vianney devoted himself untiringly to celebrating the sacrament of Reconciliation. Led by compassion for people's failings, "he spent from thirteen to seventeen hours per day in the stifling, cramped confessional. From 1827–1859 his church at Ars was never empty. Over the years the number of pilgrims increased until in 1845, 300–400 arrived daily."[9] Yet this ministry did not come naturally to him. He tried to leave Ars three times to become a Trappist monk. Once, the priests of the diocese circulated a petition that said he was not qualified to give spiritual direction. When he received the petition, he signed it! Thankfully, God's love and mercy won out, not only for the people of Ars but also for us. We too need his vision when we approach a forgiving Jesus.

Many of the saints understood the unity, peace, and service that is rooted in sacramental community, especially as experienced in the Eucharist. St. Peter Eymard (1811–1868), the founder of a religious order dedicated to Eucharistic adoration, said, "When you place a Eucharistic spark in a soul, you have implanted therein a divine seed of life."[10] St. Pius X (1835–1914), the first pope to advocate frequent Communion for children, said, "The surest, easiest, shortest way [to heaven] is the Eucharist." St. John Chrysostom encourages us by saying, Christ "nourishes us himself with his own blood and in all ways makes us one with himself."[11] And in being so strengthened we are more able to serve those around us.

After receiving Jesus in the Eucharist, we can pray not only for ourselves but for all the other people receiving the sacrament too, and those who have not yet come to the table. Together, the sacramental community can praise God, as the Book of Revelation describes:

> After this I looked, and there was a great multitude that no one could count, from every nation, from all tribes and peoples and languages, standing before the throne and before the Lamb, robed in white, with palm branches in their hands. They cried out in a loud voice, saying, "Salvation belongs to our God who is seated on the throne, and to the Lamb!" And all the angels stood around the throne and around the elders and the four living creatures, and they fell on their faces before the throne and worshiped God, singing, "Amen! Blessing and glory and wisdom and thanksgiving and honor and power and might be to our God forever and ever! Amen" (Rev 7:9–12).

Meet a Saint

St. Elizabeth Seton (1774–1821)

Elizabeth Ann Seton was born into a prominent Episcopalian family in New York City around the time of the American Revolution. She married a successful businessman and they had five children. Elizabeth enjoyed a busy social life that included dancing, theater, entertaining, Bible study, and charitable activities at her church. Elizabeth and her family fell on difficult times when her husband William became bankrupt and seriously ill. In an attempt to alleviate his illness, Elizabeth and William traveled to Italy to be in a warmer climate. William died of tuberculosis at the end of their ocean voyage. Elizabeth stayed in Italy for a time with friends. There, she discovered the Catholic Church and grew to love the Eucharist. She embraced Catholicism and returned to New York. There, she faced great persecution when she opened a Catholic boarding school. She finally took refuge in Maryland, where she established a school and a religious order, the Sisters of Charity, at the request of the bishop. She was devoted and compassionate to everyone in her care. Elizabeth eventually succumbed to tuberculosis on January 4, 1821. Before dying she exhorted her sisters: "Be children of the Church."

Reflect on the phrase "communion of saints" and what it means to you. Write about your place in the communion of saints. ∽

The declaration of feast days and the placement of saints in the Church's liturgical calendar are attempts to help us celebrate all the brothers and sisters we have in heaven. How could you acknowledge a particular saint in your life? What helps you appreciate the presence of all the saints? ∽

Prayer Sampler

St. Patrick (Fifth century)

Christ be with me, Christ before me,
Christ be after me, Christ within me,
Christ beneath me, Christ above me,
Christ at my right hand, Christ at my left...
Christ in the heart of every man who thinks
    of me,
Christ in the mouth of every man
    who speaks of me...

May the strength of God pilot us.
May the power of God preserve us.
May the wisdom of God instruct us.
May the way of God direct us.
May the shield of God defend us.[12]

Litany to the Saints

St. John of the Cross and *St. Teresa of Avila,* you supported each other in faith; help me choose the kind of friendships and community I need to grow. Pray together for me. ⇜

St. John Neumann and *Blessed Francis Seelos,* you served God together in the same rectory and religious order; help me serve Jesus alongside other Christians. Pray with me. ⇜

St. Francis de Sales and *St. Jeanne de Chantal,* you shared a deep friendship in Jesus; help me find ways to share my inmost thoughts and faith with others. Pray for me today. ⇜

Sacred Heart of Jesus, your love has been so real to so many saints—*St. Margaret Mary Alacoque, St. John Eudes, St. Maximilian Kolbe, St. Louis de Monfort, St. Faustina,* and *St. Gertrude.*

Show me how to appreciate your love. Help me stand beside them and offer myself as an instrument of your intimate love for the world. ∼ Amen.

Chapter Six

What Difference Does a Holy Friend Make?

One of the most common associations we have with saints is the granting of a miracle or receiving an answer to prayer. But there is a paradox associated with what the saints do for us. On the one hand, any good friend is always willing to help; but on the other hand, dictating a huge favor that a friend *must* do is not a good practice. And since saints are spiritual friends, it is important to realize that they do help us, but it is well to monitor our expectations in view of our friendship with them and with God. In the strictest sense (that used in the canonization process) miracles with a capital "M" are rare. They transcend the laws of nature and have no rational explanation. But we often use the term "miracle" in a wider sense, to indicate special blessings or favors that we receive in answer to our prayers. If we keep our eyes open, we can experience much help that falls into this second category, because God and the saints are always willing to help us.

In August of 1996, when my oldest son was getting married, our family preparations had reached a feverish pitch as we packed the car for the 500-mile trip from Long Island, New York to the Pittsburgh area in Pennsylvania. We planned to stop at Gettysburg and tour St. Elizabeth Seton's Shrine. My husband hesitated as he packed his guitar for a special solo during the ceremony.

"My throat is raw and I'm losing my voice," he said.

"Pack it anyway," I replied. "You might recover in the next three days."

So off we went. But John got worse and lost his voice completely; clearly, he would not be able to sing. Even though John was ill, we still needed to rest from driving, so we stopped at the Seton shrine near Gettysburg as planned. John spent his time kneeling before the altar where he placed St. Elizabeth's relic on his throat as he prayed. Only after we had driven another seventy miles did we realize that his voice had been fully restored. Whether a miracle with a capital M or not, he sang at our son's wedding after all.

In the realm of "Miracles" few saints can equal St. Vincent Ferrer (1350–1419), whose canonization process documented 873 miracles. Like Jesus, a great many of these miracles accompanied Vincent's ministry of preaching, which took him throughout Italy, Spain, Germany, and France. He usually spoke about penance and conversion. He knew that God can touch people on many levels and he became a special instrument of that touch. Vincent urges, "open the interior eyes of your soul on the light, on this heaven within you, a vast horizon stretching far beyond the realm of human activity, an unexplored country to the vast majority of human beings."[1]

The saints can be points of contact with holiness. Relating to them opens us up to the possibility of God's touch and healing. Their lives proclaim, "There is more, so much more for us! We are loved beyond our wildest dreams! We are made for wholeness; we have been blessed and can be restored!" Miracles associated with the saints draw our attention to the inner and outer transformation that is possible with God: the saints open our eyes to the light.

One of the challenges we face is recognizing that a miracle is a sign of love, a gift. We have no control over how God will show us this love and we cannot dictate what a miracle must look like.

Instead, we need to trust. We need to find ways to surrender our needs and pay more attention to God's love than to the results of our prayers. When Blessed Andre Bessette prayed for healing, he encouraged people to ask St. Joseph to intercede for them before God. Brother Andre kept the focus off himself by attributing any miracles to St. Joseph's prayers for them to God. His chapel eventually became St. Joseph's Oratory in Montreal, Quebec. Venerable Solanus Casey encouraged people to become part of the Seraphic Mass Association, and he attributed hundreds of healings to the prayerful intercession of St. Francis of Assisi and the angels. Both of these men knew how important it is to look beyond our needs, beyond miracles, and beyond the person—even the saint—who is praying, in order to keep our eyes focused on God's love.

Another challenge we often face when we pray is offering God our entire lives, not just our immediate, pressing needs. St. John Vianney often addressed this need to offer our lives to God— to become saints ourselves. Many would come to him for a word of advice, for healing, or even to snatch a piece of his clothing as a relic. They knew about the healing that was a part of his life and ministry. On one occasion an anxious woman approached St. John Vianney and asked for a relic.

"Go home and make your own!" he retorted, reminding the woman—and us—that faith in God is what counts most.

Asking for a miracle, whether it is large or small, means that we surrender some broken part of ourselves to God, in the same way that a small child places an injured hand in a parent's hand to be healed. To pray in this way is to "sacrifice" some part of ourselves to God. The challenge is to learn to offer our whole selves to God, with the help of the saints, so that the connection between us grows stronger and so that all we are and do becomes more holy.

God's Spirit has moved the saints. The ongoing presence of the Spirit in the saints is like a kind of electricity or light that clings to them and also spills out in the form of healing and spiritual gifts. In order for these gifts to be made manifest, the saints first surrendered to the Spirit's gifts—they offered themselves to be God's instruments.

St. John of the Cross referred to the Holy Spirit as a living flame of love who changes death to life. St. Edith Stein used several metaphors to describe the Spirit: "the space that surrounds and contains my being...the all-penetrating ray piercing hidden crevices, creating us anew...conquering power [in whom] everything finds its rightful place...shaping hand...sea of crystal... harmony [and] eternal jubilation!"[2] St. Cyril of Jerusalem (315–386) said, "The Spirit comes gently and makes himself known by his fragrance. He is not felt as a burden, for he is light, very light.... The Spirit comes with the tenderness of a true friend and protector to save, to heal, to teach, to counsel, to strengthen, to console."[3]

The lives of the saints give us confidence in the activity of the Holy Spirit among us. Their many charisms, graces, and virtues are like bouquets that flower because of God's presence. The good news is that God also showers us with the gifts we need to be faithful disciples like the saints. This is one of the most challenging parts of relating to the saints. It is so easy to say, "They could pray for healing, embrace the destitute, or forgive their tormentors because they were saints. They are so much better than me. I can't do what they did." But each of us is called to surrender to the Holy Spirit and to receive all the gifts that are needed to become saints. God wants to do more for us than we can imagine. We have proof in the lives of the saints that it can be done, and we, too, are called to be saints. The Holy Spirit wants to touch us and to permeate every part of our lives. The Spirit is like the sun, which is always shining whether we can see it or not. The Spirit enters our hearts at Baptism and remains with us, either like a small nightlight in a dark room or like a fire that we fan into blazing flames through prayer, sacraments, community, and the study of our faith. The choice is up to us.

All of us baptized into Christ Jesus, have been immersed in this same Spirit. God wants to shape us as we pray to and with the saints. Sometimes the Spirit will move us to new levels of conversion and we will experience spiritual healing and miracles of inner transformation. Sometimes the Spirit will grant new strength and moral healing so that we can do what is right. My grandmother would pay the saints a backhanded compliment when she was overwhelmed by a problem. She would say, "It's enough to discourage a saint with a little 's' but not a big 'S.'" Even though the saints did sometimes become discouraged, adversity and trials did not ultimately conquer them, but led them to a deeper surrender to the Spirit's activity. Many of the saints were constantly asking God for help with their struggles and repeatedly sought strength to rise above their trials, as St. Augustine so beautifully prayed:

O come, Refreshment of those who languish and faint! Come, Star and Guide of those that sail in the tempestuous sea, the world; you, only Haven of the tossed and the shipwrecked! Come, Holy Spirit, in much mercy! Make me fit to receive you. Amen.[4]

The saints offered God a willingness to bring the gifts of the Spirit to bear on the needs of others. They could focus on the Holy Spirit and the needs of others at the same time. This is not always easy. We often have difficulty bringing an awareness of God's Spirit into the arena of people's need. We can sometimes get lost in a situation and forget to use the gifts God has given us. I was reminded of this during a recent visit to St. Frances Cabrini's shrine in New York City. I spent time with St. Frances and I offered God a newly released book I had written on evangelizing children. I told God I was willing to "speak of Jesus and make Jesus known." Then I got up and went to a side chapel to light a candle. As I activated two electric "candles," a young boy named Manny charged into the side chapel and pushed the buttons on three more candles. I stopped him from lighting a whole row and told him I would show him something exciting about these candles. I quickly asked God to help me reach out to him. "We can use these candles to pray, Manny. We can use them to talk to God."

"I want to talk to her," he said, pointing at St. Frances's statue. I asked what he would like to talk to her about and he told me.

"Mother Cabrini," I said aloud, "Let me introduce you to Manny. He came here to talk to you and to ask you to help his dad and his grandmother. Be with each of them right now, wherever they are. We know, Mother Cabrini, that you loved Jesus so much. Please ask Jesus to show them his love. Thanks for listening and for this great place where we can talk to you and to God. Amen."

Manny enjoyed our prayer and left with a quick "Thank you." But I should have thanked him for the opportunity to use my own gifts of teaching, healing, and prayer. I was pleased that God had taken me up on my offer to serve. I also realized that Manny and I participated in a long-standing tradition of miracles and blessings, the graces God showers on everyone who prays. We are all "living stones" that can be used in building God's Church as we bless and serve one another (cf. 1 Pt 2:4–10). A willingness to serve is the foundation for miracles of all sorts.

> Then I saw a new heaven and a new earth; for the first heaven and the first earth had passed away, and the sea was no more.
>
> And I saw the holy city, the new Jerusalem, coming down out of heaven from God, prepared as a bride adorned for her husband (Rev 21:1–2).

Besides being actions of the Holy Spirit and the continuation of God's incarnate love, miracles are also a taste of heaven. Miracles are tiny glimpses of the new heaven and the new earth that we have been promised. Miracles are about restoring all creation to its original state. The saints are witnesses to our own destiny and give us hope in the resurrection of our bodies, minds, hearts, and souls. There is life after death. There is healing love. There is a fulfillment of persons and a flowering of gifts that is so real and pervasive that, even now, God's love spills out into our world, often through these saintly friends who can't stop themselves from loving us.

Through the resurrection of Jesus, we have been given a promise of everlasting life. That life is our goal as members of God's kingdom. Miracles are the in-breaking of God's kingdom among us. Jesus came into the world to overcome sin and death. Sickness, poverty, and global atrocities are not the final reality for Christians. Through

Jesus and his saints, we learn that we are made for everlasting life. As we head toward our home in the heavenly Jerusalem, miracles point the way to God.

Many saints had a way of seeing that went beyond sickness, poverty, fear, pollution, and wars. They could view situations and people with the eyes of Jesus. They were instruments of the Father's blessings and healing, and they expected the Holy Spirit to make these realities come to pass right before their eyes. They lived with the paradox of doing what they could while still expecting God's transforming presence. St. John Bosco cared for delinquent and homeless boys and often challenged them to faith and service to others. In 1854, St. John assigned forty-four boys to help care for cholera victims. After three months not a single one became ill with this highly contagious disease. St. Catherine of Siena was so gifted at healing feuds and touching people's consciences that three priests were assigned to hear the confessions of those she brought to repentance.

Venerable Solanus Casey had cultivated an ability to expect God's intervention throughout his life. He was first jolted into a thirst for God's presence on a rainy day when he was a young trolley driver. He found a drunken sailor standing over a young woman, whom the sailor had raped and killed. So moved by the sorrow of that event, Solanus devoted his life to prayer, service, and seeking God's healing touch for those around him. Many years later, in June 1941, a man who was struggling with alcohol addiction and experiencing the symptoms of withdrawal came to Fr. Solanus. They talked for a long time until the priest asked, "When did you get over your sickness?" The man was shocked that he used the courteous word "sickness," and that the priest assumed he was completely healed.

"You mean my drunkenness, Father?"

Father Solanus laughed, a gentle, encouraging kind of laugh. The man left and never again took a drink.[5]

In an interview near the end of his life, Fr. Solanus replied in this way to a question about his life of prayer, study, and work: "It's like starting heaven here on earth."[6] It is safe to say that he speaks for all the saints. They would encourage us on our way to holiness, and on our journey toward heaven. For we truly are on a journey and we have many saintly companions who want to befriend us, offer counsel, give us direction, and connect us to the vast communion of saints. Can't you see them standing around us? Can't you hear their voices down through the ages?

Meet a Saint

St. Katharine Drexel (1858–1955)

Katharine was born in Philadelphia to a wealthy family. She received a faith-filled upbringing and the conviction that all she had belonged to God first. Her budding love for the Eucharist was evident at age eleven when she wrote, "Jesus made me shed tears because of his greatness in stooping to me."[7] At age twelve she began to give religious instruction to the children of farm workers on her family's estate, and as a young debutante, she cared for her dying stepmother.

Katharine deliberated whether she was called to the religious life while she worked in the Native American missions. Katharine, who inherited a twenty million dollar banking fortune, built mission schools in several states with the help of her sister, and they contributed 1.5 million dollars from their inheritance. Still, Katharine wanted to do more. Her friend, Bishop O'Connor, suggested that she start a religious order for ministry to Native Americans and African Americans, and she founded the Sisters of the Blessed Sacrament. St. Frances Cabrini also encouraged her. By 1942, about 15,000 children from low-income families were receiving some of the best education available. She also founded Xavier University in New Orleans, which became the first U.S. Catholic institution of higher learning for African Americans. In 1935, she suffered a heart attack and retired from active work, but spent her remaining years in prayer.

What is your experience of small miracles or favors received from God? What does your experience and understanding of such blessings tell you about God? Think of a situation in your own life or in the life of a loved one that needs "miraculous" intervention. Talk to God and to one of the saints about this need. Then, in silent prayer, listen to what God is saying to you about the situation. ～

Imagine the saints as they live in heaven. What is your personal image of life after death? How does it affect your daily life? Talk to one of the saints that we have met together. Tell him or her about your dreams and fears concerning death and eternal life. ～

Prayer Sampler
St. John Perboyre (1802–1840)

Oh my divine Savior, transform me
    into yourself.

May my hands be the hands of Jesus.
May my tongue be the tongue of Jesus.
Grant that every faculty of my body
    may serve only to glorify you.
Grant that I may live but in you and by you
    and for you
that I may truly say with Saint Paul: "I live
    now, not I, but Christ lives in me."[8]

Litany to the Saints[9]

St. Philip Neri, you loved to tell jokes but
you were serious enough to serve God for many
years as a layman. Later as a priest you helped
ordinary people discover God; help me find my
own vocation. St. Philip, pray for me. ⌁

Blessed Josefa Naval Gerbes, you gave God
your home for the faith formation of others. You
taught women how to embroider and how to listen to spiritual reading. Help me to put my talents and all I have at God's disposal. Pray with
me now. ⌁

St. Joseph Moscati, you served God and his
people as a physician, encouraging patients to
draw nearer to God and receive the sacraments.
Help me to find ways to invite others back to

you and your Church. St. Joseph, pray for me today.

Venerable John Henry Newman, you did not give up your search for truth until it brought you to the threshold of faith. Ask God to give me the desire to learn more and more about life in the Spirit. Pray with me now. ∼

St. Ambrose, you encouraged and taught *St. Augustine.* Help me find the spiritual direction I need to be faithful to God. Help me turn to the Holy Spirit often like Augustine. ∼

> Breathe in me, O Holy Spirit,
> that my thoughts may all be holy.
> Act in me, O Holy Spirit,
> that my work, too, may be holy.
> Strengthen me, O Holy Spirit,
> that I may defend all that is holy.
> Guard me, O Holy Spirit,
> that I may always be holy.[10]
>
> *St. Augustine*

Conclusion

This book started with the announcement of St. Thérèse's historic visit to the United States through her relics. I will finish with my experience of meeting her at St. Patrick's Cathedral in New York City during that visit. A photo of St. Thérèse covered the large rose window over the vestibule where crowds of people were waiting. I slowly made my way up to the reliquary of gilded jacaranda wood, wondering what I would say or what I would ask for. Then a young woman who had wandered in from the street caught a glimpse of the church-shaped reliquary on a large TV monitor and asked me what was in it. I told her a little about St. Thérèse and she was pleased with her brief visit. I continued to move forward and pray. When I touched the case protecting St. Thérèse's remains I just smiled and said, "Thank you. Thank you for being my friend."

She is one of the reasons why I have the confidence to go on. You will also find friends along the way who will support you. We are in good company on the road to heaven, the company of all the saints. The best advice for this journey comes from St. Thérèse herself:

> This daring ambition of aspiring to great sanctity has never left me. I don't rely on my own merits, because I haven't any: I put my confidence in him who is virtue, who is holiness itself. My feeble efforts are all he wants; he can lift me up to his side and, by clothing me with his own boundless merits, make me a saint.[1]

PART TWO

Saintly
Resources

Saints and Blesseds in Our Own Backyard

The saints are the true expression and the finest fruit of America's Christian identity. In them, the encounter with the living Christ "is so deep and demanding…that it becomes a fire which consumes them completely and impels them to build his Kingdom, to the point that Christ and the new Covenant are the meaning and the soul…of personal and communal life." The fruits of holiness have flourished from the first days of the evangelization of America. Thus we have St. Rose of Lima (1586–1617), "the New World's first flower of holiness," proclaimed principal patroness of America in 1670 by Pope Clement X. After her, the list of American saints has grown to its present length…. The saints and the beatified of America accompany the men and women of today with fraternal concern in all

their joys and sufferings, until the final encounter with the Lord.

Excerpt from Ecclesia in America
(Chapter II, 15) by Pope John Paul II

From the United States

Blesseds:

Francis Xavier Seelos (1819–1867)
Redemptorist missionary to German-American Catholics

Junipero Serra (1713–1784)
Founder of early California missions

Kateri Tekakwitha (1656–1680)
Mohawk convert in pre-colonial New York

Mother Theodore Guerin (1798–1856)
Foundress of the Sisters of Providence of St. Mary-of-the-Woods, Indiana

Saints:

Elizabeth Ann Seton (1774–1821)
Episcopalian convert who established Catholic schools and founded the Sisters of Charity

Frances Xavier Cabrini (1850–1917)
Missionary to Italian-American immigrants and founder of the Missionary Sisters of the Sacred Heart

John Neumann (1811–1860)

Redemptorist missionary, named bishop of Philadelphia

Katharine Drexel (1858–1955)

Philadelphia heiress and founder of Sisters of the Blessed Sacrament

Rose Philippine Duchesne (1769–1852)

Missionary in the Mississippi River Valley

From Canada

Blesseds:

Brother André Bessette (1845–1937)
Member of the Congregation of Holy Cross, built St. Joseph's Oratory in Montreal

Dina Bélanger (1897–1929)
Member of the Sisters of Jésus-Marie

Marie-Anne Blondin (1809–1890)
Foundress of the Sisters of St. Anne

Marie-Rose Durocher (1811–1849)
Foundress of the Sisters of the Holy Names of Jesus and Mary

André Grasset (1758–1792)
A native of Montreal who was martyred during the French Revolution

Frédéric Janssoone (1838–1916)
Franciscan missionary priest

François de Laval (1623–1708)
First bishop of Quebec

Marie of the Incarnation (1599–1672)
Began the Ursuline Order in Quebec

Marie Catherine of St. Augustine (1632–1668)
French missionary to Québec

Louis-Zéphirin Moreau (1824–1901)
Bishop of Saint-Hyacinthe, Quebec

Marie-Léonie Paradis (1840–1912)
Foundress of the Little Sisters of the Holy Family

Émilie Tavernier-Gamelin (1800–1851)
Foundress of the Sisters of Providence of Montreal

Saints:

Marguerite Bourgeoys (1620–1700)
Foundress of the Congregation of Notre Dame

Marguerite D'Youville (1701–1771)
Widow and foundress of the Grey Nuns

The Jesuit martyrs:
John de Brébeuf (1593–1649)
Noel Chabanel (1613–1649)
Anthony Daniel (1610–1648)
Charles Garnier (1605–1649)
René Goupil (1608–1642)
Isaac Jogues (1607–1646)
Gabriel Lalemant (1610–1649)
Jean de la Lande (d. 1646)

Making a Pilgrimage

Why a Pilgrimage?

We embark on a pilgrimage because the journey itself has the power to build our faith. A pilgrimage is not a vacation but a retreat "on your feet," moving through the midst of the world, yet focusing your heart gently on the Lord. A pilgrimage is grounded in the need to rekindle the fire of faith. It is a spiritual adventure born of holy passion and begins with the decision to pursue God in a physical place. Preparing, traveling, sightseeing, and the return home can take on a prophetic and sacred dimension.

A pilgrim isn't just a tourist. Tourists focus on enjoying the sights and sounds of far-away places. While touring fills a legitimate need for leisure, a pilgrimage often includes ministry to others and seeing unexpected problems in a new way. Things like travel delays, poor food, and getting lost become spiritual opportunities. When we are on pilgrimage every detail can become a way to touch God. Jesus can speak to us as we travel. Companions on pilgrimage become brothers and sisters on a journey to the Father. Trials become opportunities for prayer and sacrifice.

A Tradition of Pilgrims

A thousand years before Christ's birth, Solomon's temple in Jerusalem became a site of pilgrimage for the Jews (cf. 1 Kgs 8; 2 Chr 7:8–10), who were invited to travel at three sacred times of year: Passover, Pentecost, and the Feast of Booths. Pilgrims to Jerusalem during the great annual feasts prayed, sang and reflected on the Pilgrim Psalms (120–134) as they approached the Holy City and the temple on Mount Zion.

In the New Testament, we catch glimpses of Jesus on pilgrimage along with great crowds. Pilgrimages were woven into the fabric of his family's life. "Now every year his parents went to Jerusalem for the festival of the Passover. And when he was twelve years old, they went up as usual for the festival" (Lk 2:41–42). He continued this custom as an adult (Jn 2:13, 7:2–10). Jesus treated his whole ministry as a continuous pilgrimage led by the Holy Spirit. He was always on the move: Jesus "went on through cities and villages, proclaiming and bringing the good news of the kingdom of God" (Lk 8:1).

After Jesus rose from the dead, his disciples went on a Pentecost pilgrimage to Jerusalem. At their destination they experienced the Holy Spirit in the upper room and became the Church, the Body of Christ, sent on another journey. In more recent times Pope John Paul II has been a "pilgrim pope," visiting many, many nations. His description of journeying to places made sacred by God's presence sums up the spiritual experience of a pilgrimage:

A pilgrimage evokes the believer's personal journey in the footsteps of the Redeemer: it is an exercise of practical asceticism, of repentance for human weaknesses, of constant vigilance over one's frailty, of interior preparation for a change of heart.

Preparing a Pilgrimage

As we prepare for a pilgrimage, our family spends a few weeks reading about the saint or place we will visit. Sometimes I write a short novena prayer and use it every day for nine days before we leave. We have even made plans to visit a nearby museum to help us appreciate the culture and people that nourished this holy person.

You can also use the "Pilgrim Psalms" (120–134) as a way to prepare. These ancient prayers were used by the Hebrews as they climbed the mountains on a yearly pilgrimage to Jerusalem. Use one each day in preparation for the journey.

Where do we go?

~ If you have the financial means, international destinations include the sites of Marian apparitions like those at Lourdes, France; Fatima, Portugal; or Guadalupe, Mexico. Or you can travel to Rome and the Vatican, the "heart" of the Catholic Church and site of the martyrdoms of many of the early Christians.

~ In the United States, some pilgrimage sites are the shrines of Blessed Kateri Tekakwitha, St. Frances Xavier Cabrini, the North American Martyrs, St. Elizabeth Seton, St. John Neumann, and St. Katharine Drexel. Other options for a pilgrimage are the Shrine of the Immaculate Conception in Washington, D.C.; Our Lady of the Snows Shrine in Belleville, Illinois; the Divine Mercy Shrine in Stockbridge, Massachusetts; Our Lady of La Salette in New Hampshire; and the California Missions established by Blessed Junipero Serra. For a more complete listing see *The Liguori Guide to Catholic USA* by Jay Copp (Liguori, MO: Liguori Publications, 2000).

～ A family-roots pilgrimage can be worthwhile. Experience the holy places of your ancestors and catch the flavor of their spiritual lives and times. Visiting an ancestral cemetery would also be appropriate.

～ Plan a pilgrimage to your own holy places. Where were you baptized? Where did you celebrate First Eucharist, Confirmation, or perhaps the Sacrament of Matrimony? All of these are worthy sites of personal pilgrimage and spiritual renewal.

Andrew Kim Taegon, Agnes, Bede, Alphonsus di Liguori, John Neumann

Helping Kids Make Friends with the Saints

"Saint Hunting" and Celebrations

To help a child make friends with the saints, take a tour of your parish church. While the child explores all the objects in the church, you can talk with him or her about the purpose and meaning of each object. You might share some stories about the saints who are represented in the images. When you get home, research a child or family member's patron saint, a saint you saw in church, or a saint who is related to your family's ancestral homeland. Try to involve the child in choosing a saint that he or she is attracted to, then use children's stories, pictures, or videos to learn about this saint together. Invite the child to create a physical representation of the saint, such as a drawing, mosaic, painting, or clay model.

For more ideas about faith sharing and projects suitable for children see *Evangelizing Unchurched Children* by Therese Boucher (San Jose, CA: Resource Publications, Inc., 2000) at http://www.rpinet.com/products/euc.html.

Share Visual Encounters and Faith Stories

Display artwork that portrays the saints, perhaps using small pictures and art pieces that can be interspersed with family photos. A good source of saints' pictures for children are the Holy Traders Saint cards, sets of colorful plastic-coated cards (for children and those with good eyesight).

Share your own faith stories and experiences with the saints. Talk about how a saint has helped you find God. Children are very comfortable with lots of heroes, but they do need help in sorting out the relative importance of any one hero. Any saint, and all saints, are meant to fit into the larger experience of faith in God. Celebrate the feast day or birthday of a child's patron saint, a family member's namesake, or a saintly friend that you have discovered together.

Were You There On Good Friday?

Many of us are familiar with the life of St. Francis of Assisi. One of his first experiences of falling in love with Jesus occurred in the neglected church of San Damiano. St. Francis experienced God's love while praying before a large wooden crucifix, with angels and many people painted around Jesus, including the Mother of Jesus, the Apostle John, and the centurion from Capernaum. That day as Francis imagined himself at the foot of the cross, he could hear Jesus talking to him. A very good description of this *"San Damiano Cross"* can be found by following the link on the "St. Francis of Assisi" page at www.christkey.com. An image of the cross can also be printed from this website. Then you might want to enlarge the cross and cut out the Jesus figure in the center. Ask the child to imagine finding a cross like this in an abandoned church. The cross would be called the *"St. _____ (fill in child's name) Cross."* Which holy people would they see next to Jesus? Ask them to draw familiar saints, family members who have died, angels, and whomever they would like to see next to Jesus. Most very young children would want to add themselves also. Take some time to talk to God aloud together about the final drawing

Saints Around the Globe

Begin by mounting a colorful map of the world on posterboard, then research one or two saints from each continent. For each saint collect:

- ~ a photo, drawing, or three-dimensional figure of the saint;
- ~ a short biography;
- ~ a photo of the saint's geographical area.

Find a short biography of each saint and condense it into two or three points that your child likes about the saint. A good resource for biographies is *Saints for Young People* by Sr. Helen Wallace (Pauline Books & Media, 1983). We found photographs of the saint's geographic areas in the *Encarta Encyclopedia,* and photos of some of the saints in *Faces of Holiness* by Ann Ball. You might also use an old religious goods catalogue for some pictures.

The final step is to locate on a map the geographic area for each saint and mark it with a pushpin. Then mount the three kinds of objects you have collected in clusters around the edges of the map. Yarn can be used to connect the geographic spot with the collected material about that saint. Short biographies of saints from the less familiar areas of the world can be found on the "Global Saints" page at www.christkey.com (click on author and friends to find the link).

Philip, John Bosco, Mary of Jesus Crucified, Francis de Sales, Philomena

Websites for Saintly Friends

Saints and Shrines Websites

St. Frances Cabrini Shrine in New York	www.cabrinishrineny.org
St. Faustina from Poland	www.faustina.ch
St. Katharine Drexel	www.katharinedrexel.org
St. Therese of Lisieux	www.littleflower.org
Shrine of Our Lady of Lourdes in France	www.lourdes-france.com
Shrine of the North American Martyrs	www.martyrshrine.org
National Shrine of the Immaculate Conception in Washington, D.C.	www.nationalshrine interactive.com
Padre Pio Foundation of America	www.padrepio.com
National Shrine of St. Elizabeth Ann Seton	www.setonshrine.org

Blessed Francis Xavier Seelos	www.seelos.org
The Father Solanus Guild	www.solanuscasey.org
National Shrine of St. John Neumann	www.stjohnneumann.org
St. Jude Shrine in Baltimore	www.stjudeshrine.org

Websites with Saintly Themes

www.american catholic.org	Offers "Saint of the Day" biography, e-cards, links.
www.catholic.org	Offer a listing of patron saints, along with saint biographies, FAQ about saints, daily readings, Scripture search.
www.christkey.com	saints, evangelization, life in God's Spirit.
www.cin.org	Catholic Information Network is a source of Church documents.
www.jesuit.ie/prayer	"Sacred Space" offers guided prayer experiences using your computer screen.
www.pauline.org	offers "A Saint a Day" with short biographies.
www.siena.org	The Catherine of Siena Institute. Offers a newsletter, workshops, resources, and links for people who want to discover their own spirituality and gifts.

Recommended Reading

Saint Biographies

Agasso, Domenico. *Thecla Merlo: Messenger of the Good News*. Boston: Pauline Books & Media, 1994.

Attwater, Donald. *A New Dictionary of the Saints*. Collegeville, MN: Liturgical Press, 1997.

Ball, Ann. *Faces of Holiness: Modern Saints in Photos and Words*. Huntington, IN: Our Sunday Visitor, 1998.

A collection of biographies.

Benigni, Mario and Goffredo Zanchi. *John XXIII: The Official Biography.* Boston: Pauline Books & Media, 2001.

Butler's Lives of the Saints. On CD-Rom. Fort Collins, CO: Ignatius Press.

Cristiani, Leon. *Saint Francis of Assisi*. Boston: Pauline Books and Media, 1983.

De Fabregues, Jean. *Edith Stein: Philosopher, Carmelite Nun, Holocaust Martyr.* Boston: Pauline Books & Media, 1993.

Derum, James Patrick. *The Porter of St. Bonaventure's.* Detroit: Fidelity Press, 1968.
A biography of Venerable Solanus Casey.

Fisher, Lillian M. *Kateri Tekakwitha: The Lily of the Mohawks.* Boston: Pauline Books & Media, 1996.

Fisher, Lillian M. *The North American Martyrs: Jesuits in the New World.* Boston: Pauline Books & Media, 2001.

Freze, Michael, S.F.O. *Patron Saints.* Huntington, IN: Our Sunday Visitor, 1995.

Ghezzi, Bert. *Voices of the Saints: A Year of Readings.* New York: Doubleday, 2000.

Goodlier, Alban, S.J. *Saints for Sinners.* Fort Collins, CO: Ignatius Press, 1995.

Laurentin, René. *Bernadette Speaks: A Life of St. Bernadette Soubirous in Her Own Words.* Boston: Pauline Books & Media, 2000.

Molla, Blessed Gianna Beretta. *Love Letters to My Husband.* Boston: Pauline Books & Media, 2002.

Neumann, St. John, C.SS.R. *Autobiography of St. John Neumann.* Boston: Pauline Books & Media, 1977.

Pelucchi, Giuliana. *Blessed Gianna Molla: A Woman's Life.* Boston: Pauline Books & Media, 2002.

Tarry, Ellen. *Pierre Toussaint: Apostle of Old New York.* Boston: Pauline Books & Media, 1999.

The Saints: Icons of Light and Love. Boston: Pauline Books & Media, 1998.

A multi-sensory introduction to many important historical saints.

Zanchettin, Leo and Patricia Mitchell. *A Great Cloud of Witnesses.* Ijamsville, MD: The Word Among Us, 1998.

A collection of short biographies.

Quotations from Saints

Adels, Jill Haak. *Wisdom of the Saints: An Anthology.* New York: Oxford University Press, 1987.

Quotes arranged by subject.

Chervin, Ronda. *Quotable Saints.* Ann Arbor, MI: Servant Publications, 1992.

Dollen, Charles, ed. *Prayer Book of the Saints.* Huntington, IN: Our Sunday Visitor, 1984.

Quotes and prayers arranged by date.

Chiffolo, Anthony. *At Prayer with the Saints.* Liguori, MO: Liguori Publications, 1998.

A fresh and inspiring collection of new and familiar quotes.

Dollen, Msgr. Charles, *The Book of Catholic Wisdom*. Huntington, IN: Our Sunday Visitor, 1986. A collection of quotes.

Saints and Spirituality

Boucher, John J. *Following Jesus: A Disciple's Guide to Discerning God's Will.* Pecos, NM: Dove Publications, 1995.

Practical suggestions for building a life of faith.

Boucher, Therese. *A Prayer Journal for Baptism in the Holy Spirit.* Locust Grove, IN: Chariscenter U.S.A., 2002.

Fifty days of prayers focusing on Baptism, Confirmation, and Eucharist.

DeSiano, Frank, and Kenneth Boyack. *Discovering My Experience of God.* Mahwah, NJ: Paulist Press, 1992.

A workbook with reflection questions.

Meyers, Fr. Rawley. *The Saints Show Us Christ.* San Francisco: Ignatius Press, 1996.

Scanlon, Michael. *Titles of Jesus.* Steubenville, OH: Franciscan University Press, 1990.

Prayerful reflections on the names for Jesus.

Moore, Brian, S.J. *Devotions to the Holy Spirit.* Boston: Pauline Books & Media, 1988.

Stinissen, Wilfrid. *Praying the Name of Jesus.* Liguori, MO: Liguori Publications, 1998.

A guide to prayer.

Weddell, Sherry. *The Catholic Spiritual Gifts Resource Guide.* Seattle, WA: St. Catherine of Siena Institute 1997

———*Catholic Spiritual Gifts Inventory.* Seattle, WA: St. Catherine of Siena Institute 1997

About Saints...

Cantalamessa, Raniero. *Mary: Mirror of the Church.* Collegeville, MN: Liturgical Press, 1992.

A treatment of how we are connected to Mary.

Freze, Michael, S.F.O. *The Making of Saints.* Huntington, IN: Our Sunday Visitor, 1991.

An easy-to-understand survey of interesting things about the saints.

McBride, Alfred, O.P. Praem. *The Story of the Church.* Cincinnati: St. Anthony Messenger Press, 1995.

Learn about the historical context of many saints.

Woodward, Kenneth L. *Making Saints.* New York: Simon and Schuster, 1990.

An extensive description of the canonization process.

Saint Biographies for Children

Alves, Mary Emmanuel, FSP. *Saint Francis of Assisi: Gentle Revolutionary.* Boston: Pauline Books & Media, 1999.

Bertanzetti, Eileen Dunn. *Saint Pio of Pietrelcina: Rich in Love.* Boston: Pauline Books & Media, 2002.

Charlebois, Fr. Robert, Mary Sue Holden, Marilyn Diggs. *Saints for Kids by Kids.* Liguori, MO: Liguori Publications, 1984.

De Santis, Zerlina. *Journeys with Mary: Apparitions of Our Lady.* Boston: Pauline Books & Media, 2001.

Giaimo, Donna, FSP and Patricia Edward Jablonski, FSP. *Saint Ignatius of Loyola: For the Greater Glory of God.* Boston: Pauline Books & Media, 2001.

Glavich, Mary Kathleen, SND. *Saint Julie Billiart: The Smiling Saint.* Boston: Pauline Books & Media, 2001.

Grunwell, Jeanne Marie. *Saint Elizabeth Ann Seton: Daughter of America.* Boston: Pauline Books & Media, 1999.

Heffernan, Anne Eileen, FSP and Patricia Edward Jablonski, FSP. *Blesseds Jacinta and Francisco Marto: Shepherds of Fatima.* Boston: Pauline Books & Media, 2000.

Heffernan, Anne Eileen, FSP and Mary Elizabeth Tebo, FSP. *Saint Bernadette Soubirous: Light in the Grotto.* Boston: Pauline Books & Media, 1999.

Hill, Mary Lea, FSP. *Saint Edith Stein: Blessed by the Cross.* Boston: Pauline Books & Media, 2000.

Jablonski, Patricia Edward, FSP. *Saint Maximilian Kolbe: Mary's Knight.* Boston: Pauline Books & Media, 2001.

Kerry, Margaret Charles, FSP and Mary Elizabeth Tebo, FSP. *Saint Anthony of Padua: Fire and Light.* Boston: Pauline Books & Media, 1999.

Nobisso, Josephine. *Saint Juan Diego and Our Lady of Guadalupe.* Boston: Pauline Books & Media, 2002.

Orfeo, Christine Virginia, FSP and Mary Elizabeth Tebo, FSP. *Saint Isaac Jogues: With Burning Heart.* Boston: Pauline Books & Media, 2002.

Wallace, Susan Helen, FSP. *Saint Joan of Arc: God's Soldier.* Boston: Pauline Books & Media, 2000.

List of Saints Mentioned

Bold print denotes a biography or prayer.
Vn. = Venerable, Bl. = Blessed, St. = Saint

A

St. Agnes 25

St. Alphonsus Liguori 11, 68

St. Ambrose 41, 71, 79, 80, 104

Bl. Andre Bessette 22, 92, 113

Bl. André Grasset 113

St. Anne 11

St. Augustine 42, 44, 61, 66, 72, 80, **95–96, 104**

B

St. Bartholomew 25

St. Bernadette Soubirous 45, 66–67, 71

St. Bernard of Clairvaux ix, 41

St. Bonaventure 59

C

St. Catherine of Alexandria 25

St. Catherine of Genoa 33

St. Catherine of Siena 15, 41, 59, 66, 72, 99

St. Catherine Laboure 66, 67

Vn. Catherine McAuley 77

St. Clare of Assisi 11, **52,** 80

Vn. Cornelia Connelly 77

St. Cyril of Jerusalem 72, 94

D

Bl. Damien de Veuster 48

Bl. Dina Bélanger 113

St. Dominic 44, 66

E

St. Edith Stein 25, 26, 45, 46–47, 50–51, 72, 93–94

St. Elizabeth Ann Seton 3, 5, 7, 20, 29, 35, 78, 80, 85–86, 90, 111, 118

St. Elizabeth of Hungary 46, 64

Bl. Émilie Tavernier-Gamelin 114

F

St. Faustina Kowalska 46, 87

St. Frances Xavier Cabrini 3, 8–9, 39, 57, 60–61, 80, 96–97, 101, 111, 118

St. Francis Xavier 44

Bl. Francis Xavier Seelos 80, 87, 111

St. Francis de Sales 6, 21, 24, 45, 66, 71, 87

St. Francis of Assisi 18–19, 64, 71, 80, 92, 123

Bl. François de Laval 113

Bl. Frédéric Janssoone 113

G–H–I

St. Gertrude 87

Bl. Gianna Beretta Molla 26

St. Gregory the Great 14

Bl. Henry Suso 15

St. Ignatius of Antioch 25, 58, 72

St. Ignatius of Loyola 25, 36, 65

St. Isidore 11

St. Isaac Jogues 44–45, 114

J

Bl. James Alberione 49, 54

St. Jane Frances de Chantal 23, 87

St. Jerome 23, 61

The Jesuit martyrs:
John de Brébeuf,
Noel Chabanel, An-
thony Daniel, Charles
Garnier, René Goupil,
Isaac Jogues *(see
St. Isaac Jogues),* Gab-
riel Lalemant, Jean
de la Lande 114, 118

St. Joan of Arc 25, 72

St. John Bosco 12, 99

St. John Chrysostom 61,
84

St. John Eudes 53, 87

Vn. John Henry New-
man 104

St. John of the Cross 60,
87, 93

St. John of God 11

St. John Neumann 7,
55–56, **69–70**, 80,
87, 112, 118

St. John Perboyre 58,
102

St. John Vianney 13, 42,
71, 83, 92–93

Bl. Pope John XXIII 43,
77

Bl. Josefa Naval Gerbes
103

St. Joseph 92

St. Joseph Moscati 103

St. Juan Diego 17

Bl. Julian of Norwich 60

Bl. Junipero Serra 111,
118

K–L

Bl. Kateri Tekakwitha 7,
21, 37, 81, 111, 118

St. Katharine Drexel 49,
53, 64, 80, **101–102,**
112, 118

St. Louise de Marillac
11, 72

St. Louis de Montfort
66, 87

Bl. Louis-Zéphirin Mor-
eau 114

M

St. Margaret of Antioch
25

St. Marguerite D'You-
ville 114

St. Margaret Clitherow
15, 58, 72

St. Margaret of Scotland 48

St. Margaret Mary Alacoque 65, 72, 87

St. Marguerite Bourgeoys 6, 114

Bl. Marie-Anne Blondin 113

Bl. Marie Catherine of St. Augustine 114

Bl. Marie-Léonie Paradis 114

Bl. Marie of the Incarnation 6, 113

Bl. Marie-Rose Durocher 113

St. Martin de Porres 47–48, 72

Bl. Mary McKillop 64

Vn. Matt Talbot 11

St. Maximilian Kolbe 12, 49, 66, 72, 87

St. Monica 42

P

St. Patrick 26, 66, 71, **86**

St. Paul 43, 45, 79

St. Paul of the Cross 60, 65

Bl. Pauline of Mallinckrodt 47

St. Perpetua 58

St. Peter Claver 11

St. Peter Eymard 83

Bl. Peter To Rot 49

St. Philip Neri 103

Vn. Pierre Toussaint 3, 29, **34–35**, 37, 77

St. Pius X 83–84

R–S

St. Richard of Chichester 71

St. Rose of Lima 11, 109

St. Rose Philippine Duchesne 19, 42, 112

St. Sharbel Makhlouf 73–74

Vn. Solanus Casey 6, 19, 92, 99–100

T

St. Teresa of Avila 13, 15, 25, 30, 50, 60, 67, 81, 87

Vn. Terrence J. Cooke 77

Vn. Thecla Merlo 49, 54

Bl. Theodore Guerin 111

Bl. Teresa of Calcutta 14

St. Thérèse of Lisieux ix,
   x, xi, 5, 24, 25, 32, 54,
   61, 62, 64, 105–106

St. Thomas More 11, 27,
   37, 58

V

St. Vincent de Paul 64

St. Vincent Ferrer 26, 91

Notes

Introduction

1. Jill Haak Adels, *The Wisdom of the Saints* (New York: Oxford University Press, 1987), 4.

2. Society of the Little Flower. www.littleflower .org, September 1999. < http://www.littleflower.org > .

3. *Catholic Household Blessings and Prayers* (Washington, D.C.: United States Catholic Conference, 1997), 350.

Chapter One: Meeting the Saints

1. Chicago: Missionary Sisters of the Sacred Heart of Jesus, 1944.

2. Ronda De Sola Chervin, *Quotable Saints* (Ann Arbor, MI: Servant Publications, 1992), 96.

3. *Catechism of the Catholic Church*, n. 2156.

4. *CCC*, nn. 2158–9.

5. Chervin, *Quotable Saints*, 127.

6. *Ibid*, 106.

7. William Storey, ed.; *Praise Him!* (Notre Dame, IN: Ave Maria Press, 1973), 185.

8. Msgr. Joseph B. Code, ed.; *Daily Thoughts of Mother Seton* (Emmitsburg, MD: Chronicle Press, 1960), January 9.

9. *Ibid,* February 26.

Chapter Two: Building Vital Friendships

1. Adels, 5.

2. Adels, 6.

3. Patrick Ahern, *Maurice and Thérèse: The Story of a Love* (New York: Doubleday, 1998), 140.

4. *CCC,* n. 2683.

5. *Catholic Household Blessings and Prayers,* 272.

6. Ronald Knox, trans.; *Autobiography of St. Thérèse of Lisieux* (New York: P. J. Kennedy and Sons, 1958), 289.

7. Boniface Hanley, *Ten Christians* (Notre Dame, IN: Ave Maria Press, 1979), 37.

8. *Praise Him!,* 130.

Chapter Three: The Love of Every Saint's Life

1. Bernard of Clairvaux,"The Name of Jesus," sermon on the *Song of Songs,* < http://www.stbene dictsfarm.org/19frs2.htm > .

2. Adels, 14.

3. Rev. Charles Dollen, *Prayerbook of the Saints* (Huntington, IN: Our Sunday Visitor, Inc., 1984), 170.

4. *Praise Him!*, 107.

5. Chervin, 55.

6. Adels, 81.

7. Anthony F. Chiffolo, *At Prayer with the Saints* (Liguori, MO: Liguori Publications, 1998), 5.

8. Bert Ghezzi, *Voices of the Saints* (New York: Doubleday, 2000), 210.

9. For more about her thinking read *"Edith Stein: Our Newest Saint"* by John Bookser Feister (St. Anthony Messenger Magazine Online, Oct. 1998), < http://www.americancatholic.org/Messenger/Oct1998/Feature2.asp >

10. Chiffolo, 152.

11. Ann Ball, *Faces of Holiness: Modern Saints in Photos and Words* (Huntington, IN: Our Sunday Visitor, 1998), 253.

12. Ann Ball, *Modern Saints; Their Lives and Faces*: Book 1 (Rockford, IL: Tan Books and Publishers, Inc., 1983), 375.

13. Kenneth L. Woodward, *Making Saints* (New York: Simon and Schuster, 1990), 136.

14. Margaret and Matthew Bunson, *Encyclopedia of the Saints* (Huntington, IN: Our Sunday Visitor, 1995), 2.

15. Bert Ghezzi, *Miracles of the Saints* (Grand Rapids, MI: Zondervan Publishing House, 1996), 83.

16. Ann Ball, *Modern Saints: Their Lives and Faces:* Book 2 (Rockford, IL: Tan Books and Publishers, Inc., 1990), 463.

17. Adels, 16.

18. Chervin, 142.

Chapter Four: Spiritual Mentors in Faith

1. Dollen, *Prayerbook of the Saints*, 171.

2. Mary Louise Sullivan, MSC, *Mother Cabrini, "Italian Immigrant of the Century"* (New York: Center for Migration Studies of New York, Inc., 1992), 164.

3. Chiffolo, 179.

4. Chervin, 191.

5. Adels, 56.

6. St. Frances Cabrini, *Travels of Mother Frances Xavier Cabrini* (Chicago: Missionary Sisters of the Sacred Heart of Jesus, 1944), 21.

7. As quoted in *Maurice and Thérèse: The Story of a Love,* Patrick Ahern (New York: Doubleday, 1998), 113.

8. *CCC,* n. 2684

9. Joseph F. Schmidt, FSC, *Praying with Thérèse of Lisieux* (Winona, MN: Saint Mary's Press, 1992), 74.

10. Joseph Vann, O.F.M., *Lives of the Saints* (New York: John J. Crawley & Co., Inc, 1954), 353.

11. Chiffolo, 148.

12. Chiffolo, 98.

13. Dollen, *Prayerbook of the Saints*, 155.

14. *Praise Him!,* 150.

Chapter Five: Saints Come in Bunches: The Communion of Saints

1. *CCC,* n. 828; quoting Pope John Paul II in *Christifideles Laici.*

2. Michael Freze, S.F.O., *The Making of Saints* (Huntington, IN: Our Sunday Visitor, 1991), 119.

3. You can hear this hymn at www.stmatthew-ucc.org/zzForAlltheSaints.html.

4. Performed by Point of Grace on WOW 1998: The Year's 30 Top Christian Artists and Songs, 1997, EMI Christian Music Group, Inc., World Entertainment, Inc.

5. Code, September 11.

6. Adels, 83.

7. Chervin, n. 130.

8. *CCC,* n. 950.

9. Ball, *Modern Saints: Their Lives and Faces: Book 2,* (Rockford, IL: Tan Books and Publishers, Inc., 1990), 64.

10. Adels, *Wisdom of the Saints*, 80.

11. Adels, *Wisdom of the Saints,* 82.

12. Dollen, *Book of Catholic Wisdom*, 54.

Chapter Six: What Difference Does a Holy Friend Make?

1. Ghezzi, *Miracles of the Saints,* 113.

2. *Novena to the Holy Spirit* (Wheaton, MD: The Spiritans, 1995), 17.

3. Ibid, 17.

4. Chiffolo, 49.

5. For a first person description of this encounter read James Patrick Derum, *The Porter of St. Bonaventure's* (Detroit, MI: Fidelity Press, 1968), 154.

6. Derum, 257.

7. Ball, Book 2, 457.

8. *Praise Him!,* 83.

9. Based on material from the Catherine of Siena Institute in Seattle, WA.

10. Brian Moore, SJ, *Devotions to the Holy Spirit* (Boston: Pauline Books & Media, 1976).

Conclusion

1. Schmidt, 72.

ABOUT THE AUTHOR

Therese Boucher is a religious educator and author from West Windsor, New Jersey. She presents inspirational workshops, retreats, and catechist training sessions on a regional and national basis. Her background includes ministry as a diocesan consultant, pastoral associate, puppeteer, and grant writer. Therese and her husband John are the parents of five children. For more about her books and current ministry visit www.christkey.com.

BOOKS & MEDIA

The Daughters of St. Paul operate book and media centers at the following addresses. Visit, call or write the one nearest you today, or find us on the World Wide Web, www.pauline.org

CALIFORNIA

3908 Sepulveda Blvd, Culver City,
CA 90230   310-397-8676

5945 Balboa Avenue, San Diego,
CA 92111   858-565-9181

46 Geary Street, San Francisco,
CA 94108   415-781-5180

FLORIDA

145 SW 107th Avenue, Miami,
FL 33174   305-559-6715

HAWAII

1143 Bishop Street, Honolulu,
HI 96813   808-521-2731

Neighbor Islands call: 800-259-8463

ILLINOIS

172 North Michigan Avenue,
Chicago, IL 60601
312-346-4228

LOUISIANA

4403 Veterans Memorial Blvd,
Metairie, LA 70006   504-887-7631

MASSACHUSETTS

885 Providence Hwy, Dedham,
MA 02026   781-326-5385

MISSOURI

9804 Watson Road, St. Louis,
MO 63126   314-965-3512

NEW JERSEY

561 U.S. Route 1, Wick Plaza, Edison,
NJ 08817   732-572-1200

NEW YORK

150 East 52nd Street, New York,
NY 10022   212-754-1110

78 Fort Place, Staten Island, NY
10301   718-447-5071

PENNSYLVANIA

9171-A Roosevelt Blvd, Philadelphia,
PA 19114   215-676-9494

SOUTH CAROLINA

243 King Street, Charleston, SC
29401   843-577-0175

TENNESSEE

4811 Poplar Avenue, Memphis,
TN 38117   901-761-2987

TEXAS

114 Main Plaza, San Antonio, TX
78205   210-224-8101

VIRGINIA

1025 King Street, Alexandria, VA
22314   703-549-3806

CANADA

3022 Dufferin Street, Toronto, Ontario,
Canada M6B 3T5   416-781-9131

1155 Yonge Street, Toronto, Ontario,
Canada M4T 1W2   416-934-3440

¡También somos su fuente para libros, videos y música en español!